A Soldier's Song

Ken Lukowiak was born in 1959.
He joined the Parachute Regiment
in 1979, serving in Northern Ireland,
the Falklands and Belize before
he left in 1984. He now lives in
Cornwall with his father.

A Soldier's Song
Ken Lukowiak

Mandarin

A Mandarin Paperback

A SOLDIER'S SONG

First published in Great Britain in 1993
by Martin Secker & Warburg Ltd
This edition published 1994
by Mandarin Paperbacks
an imprint of Reed Consumer Books Ltd
Michelin House, 81 Fulham Road, London SW3 6RB
and Auckland, Melbourne, Singapore and Toronto

Reprinted 1994 (twice)

A CIP catalogue record for this title
is available from the British Library
ISBN 0 7493 1642 X

Printed and bound in Great Britain
by Cox & Wyman Ltd, Reading, Berkshire

For my father
and the grandson he never holds
because of me.

Acknowledgements

These are the people who have helped me get this far. And from the first words that I wrote to these, the last, it has been far.

To Andrea, who was the first person to read 'Home, where my love lies . . .' She told me it moved her. So to prove it she cried. So I wrote some more. She's dead now, but that was her choice, so I'll remember the good times, when we drank wine.

To Clive and Jenny for being my friends through good and bad and for showing me the poem 'Absence' by Elizabeth Jennings which moved me. So I wrote some more.

To Steph for lending me that typewriter. To Alex and Joddie who laughed at 'Incoming spoons' two years before I wrote it.

To schoolteacher Jan, who corrected my spellings in wine-bars in Truro and the other Jan, who helped me believe that one day something would get published.

To Sarah and Jamie who found me when I was lonely

and took me in, and showed me love. And took me in again, and showed me love again. And again.

To Pete, Lizzy, Amy and Christopher for always being there.

To Alun Lewis for being Alun Lewis, who helped me to carry on moving forward. Thank you Alun.

To Jill and Alan. For everything. The love and the human decency.

To those people who were around me and close to me during those weeks at war. Hugh Jenner, Jed Peatfield, Frank Pye, Steve Thayer, Bill Camp, Gary Pope, Ray Canale, Chippie Chapman from the Sig's, and Andy Moodie.

To Jane, whose departure from my life drove me to such depths of insanity that all I could do was write, 'Has anybody ever written anything for you?' The final love song for you, Jane.

And finally to Sarah M., who got me through to the end after I asked 'What have I gone and done?'

Foreword

I joined the Parachute Regiment in the summer of 1979,
though for some reason nearly three years went by before
I realised it. My moment of realisation was brought
about by the exploding of an artillery shell on the
Falkland Islands. I looked up from the piece of ground
that I was trying to dissolve into and took in the
surrounding scene. I saw lots of people dressed exactly
like me, all lying down on the ground exactly like me.
Then another shell impacted, this time in the distance.
The ground exploded. Bits of soil and grass blew skywards, leaving a puff of white smoke in their wake. As I
took all of this in, it hit me like a brick. 'Oh shit,' I said,
'I'm in the Army.'

I would have thought that the six months I had spent
in basic training, not to mention the twelve months that
I served in Northern Ireland, would have given me a
slight clue to the fact that I was in the Army, but
apparently not. Of course, prior to my moment of realisation, if I was ever asked what I did for a living I would

always reply, 'I'm in the Army,' but the full implications of this statement had never quite sunk in.

Once the war was over, it did not take long for this particular insight to fade and disappear: I forgot again that I was in the Army.

The next time I remembered, I had been out of the Army for nearly seven years. A girlfriend of three years left my life. Her departure drove me to such depths of insanity that all I could do was to ask myself, 'Why?' Why was I the way I was, with my constant mood changes, my sudden outbursts of violence, my lonely moments of depression?

Then I picked up a pen. I wrote these words: 'The shelling had stopped. We got to our feet and continued to move forward.' My writings, which have now grown into this book, had begun.

All I can say of the words I have written is that they are my memories from a period of time in my life. The period of time when I was at war.

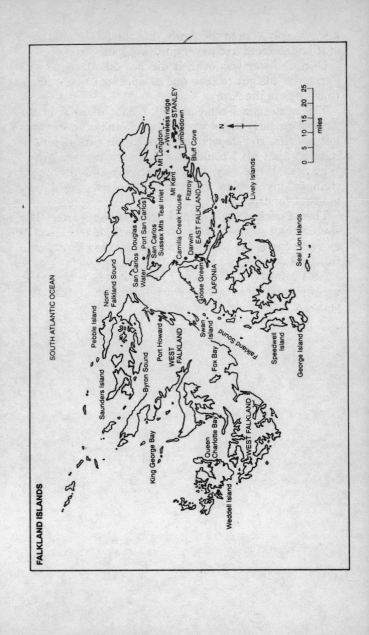

Horseless, lifeless, department store dummies (Goose Green)

We were the first to leave. I don't remember at what time. I read in a book that it was 2200 hours. I read in another book that it was 2300 hours. I don't know. I don't remember. It was dark, though – I do remember that, and I also remember why we were going.

We were going to get things going.

We left with the machine-gun platoon. We were headed for a piece of land that lay across the water to the side of the first Argentine trenches. The machine-guns were to put covering fire down on to the Argentine defenders as one of our rifle companies assaulted them from the front.

The terrain was rough; in the darkness everywhere looked the same. In broad daylight everywhere looked the same on the Falkland Islands. I remember wondering how the person leading was able to navigate. I was glad it was not a task I had to fulfil. Every so often we stopped. A blanket would be unrolled and placed over the head of the leading man. Under the blanket, with the aid of red light from his torch, the leading man checked his map. Though I still couldn't work out how he was doing it.

The place we were headed for was about five kilometres away. I read in a book that it took us three hours to get there. I read in another book that it took us four. I prefer the three-hour version. It makes me sound fitter.

When we arrived the machine-guns were set up and I and a few others were placed to the rear, facing behind, the way we had just come. We were facing behind because there's nothing more lonesome, morbid or queer than a corpse with a bleeding arse.

As we lay in the darkness, waiting for the killing to begin, I had my first real opportunity to play 'What if we were them'. If we were them we would have some men somewhere along this strip of land. This strip of land that overlooks our main defences. If we were them we would know that where I now lay was the most obvious place to put support fire down from. If we were them we would have guns ready, loaded, waiting. I looked into the darkness and wondered if there was a man looking at me, a man with a night sight, a man with a gun. I thought that even if they don't know that we're here, as soon as the first bullet leaves the barrel of one of our heavy machine-guns, then they will know. Then they will hit us. I remember thinking: What will I do? What will I do if suddenly the night around me explodes and bullets start heading my way? Return fire – that's what I'll do. Before anything – return fire. Win the fire-fight. That was one of our first lessons, one of the ones they drilled into us the deepest: before you do anything – move forward, move back or even stay where you are – you must win the fire-fight.

Our machine-guns opened up. I turned my head, looked over my shoulder and saw streaks of bright red tracer fly across the water, hit the blackness beyond and bounce skywards. I recall wondering how it was possible to know who or what our bullets were hitting. The targets seemed so far away in the darkness that I couldn't believe our fire was accurate. Firing began on the other side. The night skies lit up with flares. Voices, shouting, rang out.

I turned away from the spectacle of light and noise and looked again into the darkness and quiet that lay to our rear. Any minute now, I thought. Any minute now and all hell is going to break out around me.

Win the fire-fight, I remembered again.

Then nothing happened. Our machine-guns stopped, we lay around in the darkness for a while, daylight came and off we set, back around the water.

On the way we passed a dead horse. It was the first dead thing I had seen on the Islands.

I time flashed . . .

I was a small child again. Maybe five or six. I was wearing grey short trousers and knee-length grey socks. I was with my father and together we were looking through one of his old photograph albums. I remembered that one of the small black and white photographs held a moment in time when a pile of dead horses had lain rotting on a battlefield in France. The photograph had been taken by my father during World War II. If these words are ever published I would like my father's photograph to be printed alongside. Underneath it I would write these words: 'Some dead horses from my father's war.'

I time flashed again . . .

I was fifteen. I was wearing short grey trousers and knee-length grey socks. I was in an English literature class at school, in Kalgoorlie, in Australia. It's too hot there to wear long trousers. We were taking turns to read aloud from a book called *All Quiet on the Western Front*. The book was set during World War I when horses were still the main means of heavy transport. Some of the book's pages told of piles of rotting dead horses that once lay on another battlefield in France. I remember the way that the girls of my class became distressed as we read of dead horses. This particular book, and the film made of it, I was to remember many times over the next few weeks. My few weeks at War.

I returned to Goose Green. I found myself contemplating how the girls from my class would be feeling if they were walking with me now.

The horse on the Falklands had been killed by artillery fire. I am not sure if this artillery fire was Argentine or British, though I do know it was definitely human.

We hit a track and began to follow it forward, towards the sounds of battle in the distance. We passed a lone soldier from D Company. His name was Dave, I knew him reasonably well. He seemed different in some way, visibly shaken. Jed took a small silver hip-flask from his equipment, offered it to Dave and asked him how he was.

'Gaz is dead,' said Dave.

I had not known Gaz that well, but I still found myself remembering him. I remembered being on guard with him in Northern Ireland. I remembered playing cards with him aboard the boat that brought us here. I remembered all of the times I had spoken to him. I would speak with Gaz no more.

Gaz was dead.

A shell suddenly exploded to our right. We all took cover. It was at least 100 metres away and because it had impacted into a marsh, was of no real danger to us. Another shell landed. This time to our rear and a little closer than the first. Then another shell, this time to our front, this time much closer. They were looking for us. Another shell exploded, to our left, it was very close. Oh shit – I was sure the next one would land on top of us. Someone must have had the same thought. The order was given to move forward.

We moved off the track and cut across country towards the position Gaz had lost his life attacking. It was so

4

strange. In the distance, lying everywhere, were department store dummies, all of whom were dressed in the same grey clothing. I thought that a truck must have been carrying the dummies and as it had bumped its way across the rough terrain its load of dummies had fallen off the back. They had to be dummies because they were all so twisted. Some were lying with their arms and legs pointing skywards, others were sat up, two of them were on their knees. Yes, they were definitely dummies.

We reached the first dummy.

It was not a dummy. It was a dead man.

I know I cannot find the words to describe how I felt on first seeing the truth of war. I search my mind but I think I have forgotten. I am happy that I am unable to remember my feelings. I know that a part of me became very scared. Another part told me to shut up and get on with it. Another part gave thanks that I was still alive.

Today, as I write these words, although I cannot recall exactly how I felt, I can still see the department store dummies that lay motionless on the battlefield of Goose Green. I can still see the warped grin on the face of that first dead man. I can still be touched by the complete emptiness that surrounded his corpse.

Sometimes these memories cause my body to chill. For the briefest of moments fear flashes through my mind. My thoughts become confused and my logic becomes distorted. But don't worry – it's OK. Because then I have a drink.

'My round – what's yours Gaz?'

Hi ho, hi ho, it's off to war we go
(England)

It was a lazy weekend afternoon in April 1982. I was on leave and staying on my mother's farm at Porthtown in Cornwall. Mum wasn't home so I was alone. I was watching the TV, awaiting the start of a football match. The programme was interrupted by a newsflash. The newsflash said this: Argentine Marines have invaded and captured the Falkland Islands.

'So the fuck what', I shouted, 'get the fuck on with the football.'

After a few minutes of listening to the voice on the TV I gathered that these Falkland Islands had something to do with us. I had never heard of them and so, for some reason, thought that they must lie off the coast of Scotland.

Why not? Shetland, Falkland – sounds the same.

Argentina, on the other hand, I had heard of. The last World Cup, in 1978, had been held there.

I had always believed that Argentina, despite its large cities with their large football stadiums, was a third-world country with an army to match. But I had obviously been very wrong because there on the TV in front of me were moving pictures of Argentine soldiers running up and down the streets of an island off Scotland.

'Shit,' thought I. If they can sneak up on us from all that way away, what chance do we stand against the Russians? Before my mind could follow up this thought – i.e. hold on a minute here, I mean, why the fuck would

6

Argentina *want* to go and invade an island 8,000 miles from their home? – a map appeared on the TV screen.

'Thank fuck for that, the Falkland Islands are off the coast of Argentina.'

The newsflash continued. Apparently, for some reason beyond me, the Argentine invasion was very, very heavy news, Parliament would be recalled. In fact to help it sink in just exactly how heavy was this news, the football match I had been waiting to watch would not now be broadcast.

'Fucking Argentine bastards. I thought they bloody liked football. Someone should go and sort those shit-heads out.'

The next piece of major information via the TV was a picture of a blackboard that had been placed on a platform at London's Waterloo Station. The white chalked words told soldiers of The Third Battalion, The Parachute Regiment, to return to their barracks.

'Shit.'

Next thing I recall I'm back in Aldershot and the whole battalion (including me) is really very heavily pissed off because 3 Para are going to war and we're not – we have to go to Belize in Central America.

From the comfort of the front room of my pad in 'The Shot' I watched with envy the first ships of the Task Force set sail for the Falkland Islands.

Then, out of the blue, it's all change. The battalion's told to parade 'Scale A' (Army-speak for: 'If you're not dead, please be there'). We're all in the gym and Colonel Jones, looking like all his Christmases have come at once (whilst playing male lead in 'Debbie Does Dallas'), breaks the good news that we are going to the Falkland Islands.

Everyone cheered. Me included.

A few days later three or four of us went down to a nearby firing range to test our weapons. Well, you wouldn't want to get there and find they didn't work, would you? We travelled to the range in the OC's car. At one point there was just the OC and myself in the vehicle. I can remember saying to Major Jenner something like, 'Well, sir, this will be the end of that Thatcher woman.'

I truly did believe this, win or lose, and at that stage I didn't really think it would actually come down to fighting – just the fact that our government had allowed a third-world country to invade our sovereign territory would be the end of them. To me it was mass incompetence that our diplomats and our military intelligence had not been able to see the Argentine invasion coming. Major Jenner said he thought I was wrong. He believed Margaret Thatcher would see it through and come out of it in an even stronger position.

It's not difficult to work out why he had the pips and I didn't.

As for our 'final night' there were at least three of them and there were also at least three tearful, early-morning goodbyes with my wife Kathy's tears diminishing on each occasion. By the time we reached the farewell that turned out to be the real farewell, we both expected me to be at home when she returned from work that evening.

The real final morning came, we paraded as per normal, marched down to the square and boarded coaches that took us to Portsmouth, though it might have been Southampton. I can't remember. I could look it up in a book but from what I know about books on the subject of the Falklands War there are probably ones that say Southampton, others that say Portsmouth and I wouldn't call you a liar if you told me you had read one that said we set sail from the Baltic port of Gdansk.

When we got to the place where our ship was waiting we got off the coaches and marched down to the quay. The band played 'Don't Cry for Me, Argentina'.

And they say the Military don't have a sense of humour.

We found our allotted cabins and went on deck to wave goodbye to the flag-waving, cheering people who lined the dock below. Here's a sad thing, there was no one there to wave goodbye to me.

Kathy had already taken two days off work for the false goodbyes and she couldn't afford to take another. Anyway, it didn't really matter – nothing was ever going to come of it. We were going to get there, do a bit of sabre rattling, the Argies would piss off back to Argentina and we'd all sail home disappointed. To make me feel good, Frank's wife Bev shouted bye-bye to me. Trouble was, rather than calling me Luke, like everyone else, she had always called me 'Loopy Lou'. As she shouted this out from the quay it seemed as though everyone aboard turned and looked at me.

'Loopy fucking Lou,' said a corporal.

It took them three days to forget it. I could have killed her.

As our ship finally set sail and passed through the harbour, the sailors of the ships in dock lined the decks of their vessels and shouted three cheers. A cannon fired a salute.

It was very moving.

The ships of the Task Force that had set sail before our departure were waiting at Ascension Island for us to catch up. We arrived during the night. The following morning I went out on to the deck to smoke a cigarette. I couldn't believe outside. For as far as the eye could see there were ships. I walked around the deck to look at the view from the starboard side. It was the same as the port. Ships everywhere. I would never have even dreamed that we as a nation had so many. I suddenly realised that someone, somewhere, was taking all of this very seriously. Someone somewhere meant business.

I wasn't wrong.

We are sailing
(MV *Norland*)

The soldiers of the Task Force who arrived at Ascension Island before us disembarked from their ships and went onto the island to train and use the ranges. (Swim and sunbathe.) Because of our late arrival we did not leave the *Norland* except to practise disembarkation drills on to landing craft, and to sail around the bay, which as it turned out proved to be a very wise thing, as it was via landing craft that we eventually arrived on the Falkland Islands. We also practised disembarkation drills via helicopters which at one point were odds-on favourites to be our means of transportation on to the Islands.

The majority of the time on our journey south was filled with various forms of training. Fitness sessions consisted of PT held on the helicopter pads and running lap after lap around the *Norland*'s deck. The noise of stamping boots was a constant sound during daylight hours. The mood amongst us during these PT sessions was happy and the training was carried out with good humour. There was no need to bully or beast people into effort. The effort came from within, it was in our own interests to work hard, to push ourselves. We also had various lectures: on identifying Argentine military hardware, combat first-aid (wise move that one) and films on what to do if you were captured.

I loved the films. If they could be released for general viewing, I'm sure they would play to packed houses. The 'what to do if you were captured' movies were American-made and dated from the Korean War. After watching these films on procedure to be carried out when doing a five-stretch in an Indo-Chinese prisoner-of-war camp, the Argentines would have stood very little chance of converting us to Communism had we been captured.

At one of the lectures, one of the lance-corporal 'intellectuals' of our intelligence section warned us not to carry any mail or personal photographs on to the Islands. We were told that if we were captured with mail in our possession, the evil Argentines would be able to write home to our families and give them a blow by blow account of the torture we were receiving. Fair enough – sound advice. I could see the reasoning behind it (although all of us ended up completely ignoring it).

As for the one about not carrying photographs, I've heard some shit in my time, but they excelled themselves with that one. We were told that if the Argentines got hold of pictures of our mothers, wives or girlfriends they would be able to retouch the prints and turn them into hard-core pornography. Pictures of donkeys up your mum's bum with which they could then torment us. Someone asked if we would be able to buy the negatives.

I laughed so hard I fell off my chair.

A drill that we practised again and again aboard the *Norland* was Submarine Alert. We had all been instructed to keep a full set of clothing and anything else we might fancy carrying, should we have to abandon ship, in a black plastic bin-liner. On hearing over the ship's tannoy the words 'Submarine Alert' the idea was to walk at a calm pace (run very quickly) to your cabin, grab your plastic bag, put your helmet on and lie down on your bed. It wouldn't have been too bad if they had let us practise the lying down on beds, holding bags, with helmets on for a couple of hours. But they didn't, after a few minutes it was always back to what we were doing. In the Army there is nothing as satisfying as laying on your pit doing nothing. After a time the Submarine Alerts became something of a pain, i.e., you're holding a

11

full house, three others are still in the game and 'Submarine Alert' blasts out over the tannoy.

On one occasion we had a Submarine Alert and it was not an exercise. I was walking through a corridor at the time. When the voice on the tannoy said, 'This is not an exercise,' the pace of the soldiers around me rapidly picked up. It turned out to be a false alarm, but not to worry, at least we got a decent lie down.

While aboard the *Norland* news came through that the Argentine ship, the *General Belgrano*, had been sunk. Over 1,000 men sank, jumped, fell or were pushed into the freezing South Atlantic sea. Three hundred men died. Most of them drowned, though some of them froze.

I have a video at home. It tells the story of the Falklands War. On the video there is a scene where the news of the sinking of the *General Belgrano* is announced to some soldiers of the Task Force. The said soldiers are Royal Marines. They are in a bar, aboard the ship that is carrying them to the Islands and eventual war. On hearing the news the men around the bar become visibly saddened. They listen in silence. It hits home just exactly what they are caught up in.

When the news of the sinking of the *Belgrano* was announced over the tannoy to us Paratroopers of the Second Battalion we all cheered. It was party time. Open the bars. 'That will teach the fuckers to mess with us, a thousand less of the bastards for us to worry about' – that was our attitude.

Despite the group's apparent pleasure at the deaths of so many of our enemies, as individuals our thoughts were different. I heard many people in times of quiet reflect upon the tragedy of the loss of so many lives. We all thought that drowning in a cold sea must be a horrible way to die. It made us notice that we were also aboard a ship and that our ship was also heading towards the place where ships were being sunk.

The sinking of the *Belgrano* also brought about

another realisation. It was this: the stakes had now been raised, and it was us who had done the raising.

We had asked the Argentines, 'What have you got? We think you're bluffing.'

Two days later the Argentines showed they were not bluffing. They showed us what they had. Exocets. They sank the *Sheffield*. Twenty men died.

Aboard the MV *Norland* no one cheered.

Confessions of a nicotine addict
(MV *Norland*)

On the ship I shared a cabin with three others. The cabin was one of the better ones, situated above sea level on the top deck. It was not too small and it had its own toilet and shower. The four of us slept in two bunk beds, which lay parallel to each other along the cabin's two side walls.

Each morning we were pulled from our sleep by the ship's tannoy. One morning, while lying in bed, wiping the sleep from my eyes, I looked across to Andy, the soldier who slept in the bottom bunk opposite.

Andy was lying on his back with his eyes closed, quietly giving his own opinion as to the parenthood of the sailor on the tannoy. Still with his eyes closed, he dropped his left hand out of the bed and began to touch-search the cabin floor. His hand quickly found what his mind was looking for – nicotine.

The nicotine came in the form of one packet of Players

No.6 King Size cigarettes plus a red disposable cigarette lighter. He pulled the cigarettes and lighter up to his chest, brought his right hand out from under the bed-clothes and, still with his eyes closed, took a cigarette from the packet and lit up. The first inhale resulted in some mild coughing.

I was absolutely amazed. I was a smoker, but there was no way I could light up that early in the day, certainly not before a drink and definitely not while still in bed. I had the thought that my life was better than Andy's because I had no need to light a cigarette before getting out of bed. I was judging Andy for smoking so early, it helped me somehow come to the conclusion that I was a better person. He was doing wrong and I was not.

This is my clearest memory from that period of time. The period of time in which I sailed towards war. Only this morning as I lie in my bed and reach for my cigarettes and then cough with the first inhale, I remember the way I once sat in judgement of Andy.

As a memory – it teaches me a lot.

All quiet on the southern front
(MV *Norland*/San Carlos)

We were to land tonight. I didn't know what to expect, I don't think anyone did. The only images in my mind were replays of old war movies, moving pictures of soldiers being machine-gunned as they waded through water.

Except for one thing, I have no real strong memory of that day. I remember a lot of hurrying up and waiting and I know that I endlessly checked my equipment and cleaned my weapon, but I can't seem to remember a whole day. I can recall being in my cabin and then being in the ship's restaurant eating fried-egg sandwiches and drinking tea. I remember waiting in one of the ship's bars to be called down to the loading deck and the waiting landing craft. I recall how everyone struggled to lift up and put on their bergens, and the way everyone was worried that we were too heavy. I can still see the back of the soldier in front of me as we walked down through the red, dimly-lit ship – red so as not to impair our night vision. I remember stepping across the perilous gap that separated me from the landing craft, being careful of my every movement, knowing that a slip into the cold night waters with the load that I carried would mean certain death.

My only really strong memory from that day is of the quiet, I still hear it today. It was a very quiet day aboard the MV *Norland*.

Years later, the TV said that we all wrote our last letters home. I don't remember. I don't think that I did and I have no memory of others writing. Maybe the TV lied.

Who knows? Who cares?

The last man was loaded into the landing craft. The sound of the engine revs changed. We began to move slowly through the water. From the dark distance came the sound of shelling. The ships of the Task Force were softening the beach. I tried to push from my mind the thoughts of old war movies, I tried not to think that we could face an opposed landing, that the beach could be mined, that barbed-wire and other obstacles could block our way. I don't know how long a space of time we filled on the landing craft, all I do know is this: I never felt bored.

The landing craft slowed, its bottom scraped the sand. The ramp began to lower. We stopped. A single shot rang out in the craft. Someone had had a negligent discharge. There goes a month's pay for him, thought I. The marine at the front of the landing craft quietly called out: 'Troops out.'

Was he mad? There was still water out there. He repeated his command. 'Troops out.'

No one moved. The marine had no chance really, he did not know the magic word. The one that makes the paratroopers move. But he knew a man who did.

'Go.'

We began to pour out of the craft and into the freezing water. I remember feeling lucky; I was tall, the water didn't quite reach the bits it was better to keep dry. The machine-guns, barbed-wire and obstacles of my mind proved to be just that; of my mind. Our landing was unopposed.

All I remember then was chaos. Hundreds of men on the small strip of beach all wandering around in pitch darkness whispering questions: 'Who's that? Do you know where C Coy is?'

I bumped into Jed and stuck to him. The two of us left the beach and moved up to a track that ran above it. It was very dark. I was feeling very unsure. To my right, further along the track, I saw two men. They were both wearing bright white balaclavas. They were both carrying weapons. They weren't two of us, they couldn't be, so who were they? I wondered if I should open fire. Covering them with our weapons, we began to move slowly towards them as they moved towards us.

'Who are you?' whispered Jed.

'We're SBS. Who are you?' asked one of the white-hooded men.

'We're 2 Para,' replied Jed.

'2 Para. Fuck. You're not supposed to land until

tomorrow. We're here now recceing the beach for your landing.'

This news horrified me. My mind began to play the old 'what if' game: what if there had been Argentines on the beach? What if they had shot an anti-tank rocket through my landing craft? What if machine-guns had opened up on us as we waded helplessly through the water? What if etc., etc., etc. I called an end to my mind games by telling myself that all was well that ends well.

It later turned out that the conversation Jed had held with the two white-hooded SBS men had not been unique. It seemed nearly everyone had the same story to tell and nearly always the stories went almost word for word like ours. This now causes me to wonder if the Special Boat Service had not been playing one of their little jokes on us. If so, I didn't find it very funny then and I don't find it very fucking funny now. If, on the other hand, they had not been joking and they really had been recceing the beach for our landing, then what I want to know is how come I never got an invite to the execution of the bastard responsible for landing me on an un-recced beach. I shall probably never know the answer and, anyway, I probably don't really want to know.

All's well that ends well – remember?

After a while daylight broke and some form of order was restored. We began to march in single file towards the base of Sussex Mountain. I'll be honest now and say that I've done a few marches in my time, marching is one of the things you really do do a lot of in the paras, but that march from the beach at San Carlos to the top of Sussex Mountain was the worst. I can remember crossing a stream, quite early on, and being helped by another of the white-hooded men who was stood in the water, helping to steady passing soldiers. I asked the man in the white hood how long he thought it would take us to reach the top of that high thing over there – I pointed at the mountain.

'Well, it's about five clicks [five kilometres] so I would say about five hours.'

Five hours. Fucking stupid glorified hat wanker. Five fucking hours to do five clicks. It might take you and the rest of your bum-boy buddy marines five hours. Not us, mate. We're fucking paratroopers, haven't you heard? (I thought this by the way – I didn't actually say it.)

Next scene in the war movie starring me, it's four hours later, we've covered four clicks and I'm mentally running through my letter of apology to the marine of the SBS. The march really was turning out to be a nightmare.

Compared to others who marched that day my load (about eighty pounds) was relatively light. The fact that we had started with a slow wade through freezing sea water had done nothing for our feet and as the march progressed the constant squelching in our boots began to take its toll.

Along the way I can remember passing the padre, and then passing the padre and then passing the padre again. He had been running up and down the marching line assisting and encouraging struggling soldiers, though I never once heard him bully. There's one who's read his bible, I thought, now which part of it is it in? It's something Jesus said so it's go to be in the New Testament, and it's a parable so that cuts it down to the Gospels, but the Gospel according to whom? If I was in Ladbrokes and I had to bet on it (and if I was in Ladbrokes I surely would have to bet on it) which one would I go for; Matthew, Mark, Luke or John? Oh well, I'm called Luke, I'll go for the name, good a way as any to pick a horse. I would bet on Luke. – I looked up from my squelching feet and we had covered another few hundred yards. This was how the march went for me. I tried not to think about it, I gave myself problems to solve, options to choose.

I remember at one point looking at Jimmy, the soldier

marching in front of me. I looked down to the ground to check my footing and then back up again at Jimmy. He was gone. Vanished into thin air. A few steps further and I saw him again. He was in a ditch, up to his chest in water and cursing loudly. I don't think ditches filled with water were his thing. We pulled him out and he straight away stripped and changed his clothing. I was very happy that he had found that one for me.

Eventually we reached the base of Sussex Mountain and after a short rest we began the ascent. As we climbed I found it harder and harder to distract my mind from the task in front of me. The top of the hill seemed to get further away the more we climbed. I became pissed off. Really severely pissed off.

Out of nowhere an Argentine Mirage fighter jet screamed overhead. As the jet disappeared over the horizon I remember thinking: It's true, there really are Argentines on this island. Of course I already knew this, but seeing is believing and then you can really let your mind go to town on the consequences.

Halfway up my mountain of penance a British helicopter landed in front of us. One of its occupants leaned out and shouted:

'Can we give you chaps a lift?'

Major Jenner shouted a reply: 'Are you sure? We wouldn't want to put you to any trouble.'

Are they sure? Are they fucking sure? You mental bastard, I thought. We're all dying halfway up a fucking mountain, these guys want to save us and all shit for brains with the pips can say is, 'Are you sure?' I could see by the faces of Jed and the others that they were just as horrified by Major Jenner's reply as I was. I had the thought that any more comments like 'Are you sure?' from him and I was going to witness a re-enactment of the last scene from the movie *Caesar – The Final Days*.

The helicopter man said he was sure and it was no

trouble at all. We piled aboard the small chopper and after a bit of map pointing to the pilot we lifted off.

'I love the RAF,' said Jed.

'I love them too, sir,' said I.

After a short flight the chopper landed. We all got out and waved our thanks and farewells to the crew and Major Jenner checked his map. After a quick examination he announced that we had been dropped in the wrong place.

'I fucking hate the RAF,' said Jed.

'I fucking hate them too, sir,' said I.

In the end it turned out that things were not that bad: true, we had been dropped in the wrong place but it was a wrong place above, not below. After a short march back down the hill we found the space we were meant to fill. We unstrapped the shovels from our packs and dug in for the very first time on the Falkland Islands.

But it wasn't to be the last – not by a long way.

Bomb me now, bomb me please
(Sussex Mountain)

We were dug in on Sussex Mountain. Below us, in San Carlos Bay, the ships of the Task Force were silently singing a new song:

'Bomb me now, bomb me please.'

Their calls were soon heard. A radio operator shouted, 'Air-raid warning red.'

Trying not to show any form of panic I made my way

slowly to my trench, put my helmet on and awaited the arrival of the Argentine Air Force.

As the days had passed we had grown accustomed to air attacks on the ships in the bay and had also come to the reassuring conclusion that the jets had not flown all the way from Argentina to drop their bomb loads on little old insignificant us. Insignificant or not, we couldn't help but notice that the ships (i.e. Our Side) were coming a very bad second to the Argentine jets. If the Argentine Army was half as crazy as the Air Force then we could have a problem.

From out of nowhere two jets zoomed over my head; flying wing to wing they followed the contours of the hill down to the water's edge. They levelled out on reaching the water and flew straight towards a ship. I can recall thinking, as I watched the two jets, that there was no way the ship was going to survive. My mind told me to be prepared to view its destruction. The two jets released their bombs, the ship took at least four direct hits.

Then – nothing happened.

There were no explosions and the ship, to everyone's amazement, was still floating. I found myself feeling grateful that I was not aboard a ship in the bay. At least on the ground you could have a little panic-attack if you so wished and go for a run. On the ships, you could do nothing but pray.

During that first week on Sussex Mountain, we had not seen one British aircraft. We were told that the Argentines were receiving heavy casualties for their troubles and that on the way to the Islands, and also on their return flights, they were having to run the gauntlet of our Harriers.

All I can recall seeing, as far as Argentine Air Force casualties were concerned, was one jet which was shot down over San Carlos waters. We were also told that because the loss of their jets was so high, their aircraft were returning to different bases from the ones they had taken off from. They were doing this, we were told, so that pilots returning from bombing missions would not be able to tell the pilots yet to fly just how certain a death faced them at the hands of the British air defences.

Since my days of sitting on Sussex Mountain, watching wave after wave of Argentine fighter jets attack our shipping, I have read many accounts of the war as told by Argentine fighter pilots. It is never mentioned that they returned to different bases after their missions. I think this has something to do with the fact that they didn't. Someone on the Falkland Islands was telling us little white 'Porkies'.

But I don't mind because I liked to believe them.

Last night I had the strangest . . .
(Sussex Mountain)

We were in the playing-fields of my infant school in Swindon. We had just arrived. We knew the Argentine jets would come soon. We were digging in – digging in real quick.

I was in a panic.

I had just married and Kathy would be arriving soon. I needed to dig a bigger trench. A trench to hold two. I looked up from my half-completed hole and noticed that everyone else had finished digging. They were all in their trenches, helmets on, looking skywards.

I dug faster.

Someone called me. I looked up from my hole to see

who. Looking down on me were two soldiers. I don't remember who. Though I do remember that I didn't like them and that they also didn't like me. They asked if I needed a hand. I said, yes please, I did. They jumped in with me and began to help to dig. One of them asked where the mattress for my wife was.

I panicked some more.

I had forgotten to get a mattress for Kathy. I told the two soldiers that I needed to get a mattress and would they please carry on digging for me. They said they would. I left.

I ran across the football field, across the tarmacked playground, past a wooden climbing-frame and into a classroom. It was the classroom in which I had spent my first year at school. Inside, all of the little chairs and little desks were stacked up against the far wall. The space they had once filled was occupied by military stores. Behind a wooden table sat Frank and Yank. I explained to them that Kathy was due at any moment and I needed a mattress for her to sleep on. Frank gave me a bollocking for not drawing the mattress earlier. He told me I should 'get a grip', start 'switching on'. If it had been for me I could forget it, but as it was for Kathy he would allow me to have one. Yank went to pull one from the pile and Frank started to fill out a 1033 for me to sign for the mattress on. He couldn't find any carbon paper. He asked Yank if he had seen any. Yank said he hadn't.

I panicked even more. The jets would arrive soon, Kathy would arrive soon. Would they please hurry.

They couldn't find any carbon. Frank said not to worry, he would write it out twice. He started to write. Yank stopped him and asked if mattress didn't have only one 't'. Frank said no it had the two. I said would they please hurry. Frank and Yank began to argue on the spelling of mattress. Yank said he would get a dictionary.

I had had enough. I grabbed a mattress and ran from the classroom. Frank and Yank shouted behind me.

When I got back to my trench the two soldiers had finished the digging. I threw the mattress into the trench and jumped in on top of it to level it out along the bottom.

'Hello, Ken.'

I looked up. Kathy was there. She was wearing a nightdress. In her right hand dangled the Winnie the Pooh bear that I had bought for her birthday. Kathy climbed in with me and we lay side by side on the bottom of the trench.

The jets came.

As the bombs began to fall and explode I rolled over and lay on top of Kathy. There was a loud explosion.

I awoke.

The night was still dark. Everyone else was also awake. In the waters of San Carlos Bay below the night glowed. One of the ships was burning brightly. It turned out that the ship, HMS *Antelope*, had been hit by an Argentine bomb during an air-raid earlier that day. The bomb had not exploded. As we slept a bomb disposal man had tried to defuse it.

He failed.

The bomb exploded.

The man died.

The noise that pulled me from my sleep pushed him into his.

Night, night. God bless.

I eat, I shit, I am (1)

On the night we left the *Norland* and landed on the Islands, we took it in turns to go below to the restaurant deck. There, a hot plate, eggs, white sliced bread and both types of sauce (red & brown) were made available to us. As I picked an egg from its carton and cracked it over the hot plate I had the thought that I had been here before. In Northern Ireland every cookhouse I had ever seen always had a hot plate, eggs and white sliced bread so that soldiers going out or coming in from night patrols could go to work on an egg. As I fried my egg aboard the *Norland* I wondered if being given the opportunity to eat fried-egg sandwiches and laying your life on the line went hand in hand.

If ever you are in the British Army and suddenly a large amount of eggs for frying becomes available, take my advice – go AWOL.

The majority of the time on the Falkland Islands we lived off Army ration packs. These always came in four or five different varieties, marked 'A', 'B', 'C', etc. Normally we would draw two or maybe three packs from the stores at a time, always being careful not to land ourselves with three 'A's or three 'B's or whatever.

The ration packs that we ate from during the Falklands campaign were of the Arctic type. I had never seen an Arctic ration pack before and as I ripped into the contents of one for the first time I found myself making little 'Ooh' and 'Aah' sounds with every new discovery. There were loads of choccies.

There was also definitely more food in an Arctic pack than in our usual ones. But it did have two minor little drawbacks: all the food was dehycrated and needed to be cooked to be eaten and, even worse, the food needed so much water to *re*hydrate it that really it would have helped if we had been connected to the water mains.

Water is very important. This is one of the many perfectly obvious facts of human existence that I had been completely ignorant of before I joined the Army.

You may think that acquiring water on a place like the Falkland Islands would not fall into the category of one of the world's most difficult things to do; after all, it does piss with rain all day almost every day. Except of course when it's snowing. There's water everywhere you look.

There is also sheep shit everywhere you look. If we drank the water on the Falkland Islands untreated we became very ill. Even when we did treat it by boiling it and 'puri-tabbing' it, we still became very ill.

Eating (scoffing in para-speak) is obviously very important. Not only from the point of view that if you don't eat you die, but also because there is nothing like a good scoff to lift the old spirits when life is a piece of shit.

One of the meals in the Arctic ration packs was shepherd's pie. Though it wasn't really a pie as it consisted of a vacuum-packed sachet of instant mash and another vacuum-packed sachet of instant meat and veg. We would normally leave the main meal of the pack until last thing in the day. It helped warm us up for beddie-byes. The first time that I put together the instant shepherd's pie some shithead behind the wheel of a Skyhawk fighter jet flew overhead and in an attempt to put as much distance between myself and the sky as possible I knocked over my mess tin.

When I did finally manage to get to eat some of the shepherd's pie I was, on two counts, very happily surprised. Firstly, there was lots of it, and secondly, it tasted really nice.

I should have known it was too good to be true.

The more you ate, the worse it became. It seemed to lose its taste. Its texture became different. It got stodgy. It dried up on you. We learned very early on that the best way to approach this stuff was to scoff it down your throat as quickly as you could and hope you managed to get it all in before it turned back into powder.

In the Arctic ration packs, as with all other British Army ration packs, there was a good supply of hard-tack biscuits. Or to use their correct title, 'Biscuits AB'. Besides having the quality of filling the largest of hungry spaces they also act to block you up. In other words, if you eat loads of hard-tack you don't go shittin' a lot.

Because of the hard-tack I had eaten, I had been on the islands for nearly four days before I had my first shit. Some group of switched-on soldiers had dug a large trench over which a pole bench had been constructed for the resting of arses.

As I sat on the pole, next to another who was also shitting, looking down at the still-burning ships in San Carlos Bay, I remembered *All Quiet on the Western Front*. It's a war book. But not really. Really it's a peace book. Some of the book's pages tell of soldiers who had once shat together on toilets that had no partitioning. As a schoolboy I could not think of a time when I had ever shat in company. I had always shat alone. In a room that was locked. The thought of having to shit with someone doing the same thing twelve inches away disgusted me. It was revolting. Other pages in the book tell of killing, death, waste and all-round mass male stupidity. When I was fifteen, I thought these things were sad, but not as sad as having to shit next to someone else.

As I shat in front of someone else during my war, I laughed at the boy who had once been disgusted at the thought of what I was now doing. I thought that I had grown up.

Today, if I read *All Quiet on the Western Front*, it's the

27

killing, death, waste and all-round mass male stupidity that disgusts me. Revolts me. I think again and conclude that maybe now I really have grown up.

Maybe.

I once read in another book of a tribe that lives in Africa. They find nothing strange in shitting in front of each other. They do it all the time. But eating, they never do that in company. They find the spectacle of others pushing food into their mouths disgusting. It revolts them.

In the tribe that I was once a member of we didn't care. We ate in front of each other and we shat in front of each other.

Savage – or what? No, just practical.

Satellites of love?
(March to Goose Green)

We had now been on the Islands for almost a week. Our war had so far consisted of watching the Argentine Air Force bomb the shit out of our Navy.

Someone decided to change the situation.

On the evening of 27 May, after one false start the previous day, we left Sussex Mountain and set off for a place they called Goose Green. By the time all the companies had got into the right order and we began to march, darkness was upon us. Most of the way we followed tracks. We had left our packs on Sussex Mountain and so our loads were not as heavy as they had been on the march up from the beach head.

Every so often we would stop and rest. From these rests I have three distinct memories. I do not recall in which order they fell, but I do recall them falling.

I remember us stopping and all sitting down and leaning back to rest our weight. Frank Pye, who was marching somewhere behind me, came running forward and grabbed a figure that was sitting up the line to my front. Frank pulled the other man to his feet by his collar and asked him what the fuck he thought he was doing stopping.

This proved to be a slight error on Frank's part. The man who he had just grabbed and pulled to his feet was none other than our OC – Major Jenner. Major Jenner, fearing for his life at the hands of The Pye, began to call out: 'Colour, it's me, the OC. I'm a major. I'm allowed to stop.'

Frank then turned on me and the others and told us to shut the fuck up laughing. He then spent the next few minutes apologising to Major Jenner, who in turn spent the next few minutes telling Frank it was all right, he understood, there was no need to apologise.

On another rest stop, the soldier to my left, who was ahead of me in the marching order, tapped me on the shoulder and passed down a message. He said, 'Has anyone dropped an IWS? Pass it on.'

I had not been issued an IWS night sight, so I tapped the shoulder of the soldier to my right and began to pass the message on. Then I had a thought: just hold on a minute – if someone at the front of our human snake has found a night sight, how the fuck could it be possible for someone behind him to have dropped it? I tapped the shoulder of the soldier to my left and explained my theory.

'Oh, yeah. You've got a fucking point there, Luke.' He then tapped the shoulder of the soldier to his left and passed on my conclusion. To this day I don't really know if a night sight was actually ever dropped or found. It may have been someone's idea of a joke. If so it worked. I laughed.

Still later, we stopped and I leaned back and looked up to the heavens. The night was cloudless. The pitch-black sky held thousands of bright shining stars. As I looked I saw three very large, very shiny, bright stars. Not only were they very large and very bright, they were also moving. I pointed out the stars to the soldiers around me. Someone said that they were not stars; they were satellites. Wow! I thought. Satellites! As I stared up at the eyes in the sky I gave them a little wave. Then I sang a song to them: 'Bong, bong, bong, satellite of love.'

Some time afterwards the battle began: the stars and satellites were replaced by bright red tracer, flashes, flares; the quiet darkness was punctured by shouts, explosions, machine-gun fire.

Daylight came, and with it came our first encounter with death on the Islands, the death of Gaz, and the department store dummies.

Meanwhile, I imagined the satellites continuing their lonely orbit of the planet: I think I was stretching it a touch on the love bit.

Lost boys and junkies
(Goose Green)

We caught up with B Company – well, their casualties anyway. The battalion's medics had constructed a small circular wall made from peat in which the wounded lay. Lying away from the wall, on their own, with the whole world trying really hard to ignore them, were two bodies. They were covered by a groundsheet. Protuding from the groundsheet were four boots, a right, a left, another right and another left. Above the four boots were four khaki brown puttees and above the four khaki brown puttees were six or so inches of green denim.

They wore the same boots, puttees and denims as me. They were our dead. I wondered who they were. On the one hand I was trying not to notice them and yet on the other I wanted to go over and lift the groundsheet.

I had no morbid wish to look at dead men. Just wondered if I knew them – that's all.

An Argentine Pucara appeared on the horizon to our front. It was heading our way. All of us automatically lifted our weapons and welcomed the aircraft with a hail of bullets. As the plane flew directly overhead we all dived to the ground and buried our faces into the earth. I waited, hoping for nothing. No bomb. No napalm. No explosion. No death. Even no leaflets saying: 'Go home Tommy. Hold on to your life.'

There was nothing. The aircraft banked away to the right and disappeared over a hill. I quickly forgot the things I had just promised God and climbed to my feet.

The next thing I remember, Bill and I were running up a hill that lay to our front, heading towards one of the

Anti-Tank Platoon who had been hit by several pieces of shrapnel from a mortar round. I don't recall whether someone ordered us to go, or asked us to go, or if we went on our own initiative. On reaching the wounded anti-tanker it would be fair to say that he appeared not to be having the best of days. He seemed mainly to have been hit on the right side of his body, with most of the bleeding coming from his arm.

He was breathing quickly, very loudly. His lips were open. His teeth were clenched.

One of our medics, who had reached him before us, unwrapped a morphine syringe and punched it hard into the wounded soldier's left leg. The wounded soldier didn't even blink. Neither did the medic. I bloody did.

A large 'M' was then drawn on the wounded man's forehead and a tag that came as part of the morphine package was filled out and tied to the top button of his smock. This was to let the doctors to the rear – whom we hoped he would eventually reach – know that he had already been given morphine.

At the same time a quick examination of his wounds was made, a few shell dressings were applied and the conclusion was drawn that he could bleed away at the rate he was bleeding for a little while longer.

Someone then took the poncho from the wounded man's equipment. It was unwrapped, spread out on the ground and he was laid upon it. We all took a corner, lifted him up and then ran with him back down the hill towards the circular peat wall.

On reaching the wall we left him with a medic and then began to rifle his equipment. He carried the same weapon as Bill and I so we split his four ammunition magazines between us. His food (mainly sweets) we divided between the four of us who had carried him. He still had two nearly full water bottles so we topped up our own bottles from one of his and left him the other one. One of us didn't have a watch, so we took his. The watch was Army issue. If it had not been, it would not have been taken. Besides there was only one type of time for him now – goin' home time.

Lucky, lucky, lucky bastard.

Bill and I then took off back towards where we had last seen Major Jenner and Jed and co. They weren't there. Bill then stated the blatantly obvious: 'They're not fuckin' here, Luke.'

Our initial response was one of, 'Well thank you very fucking much. It's nice to know you're wanted.' Then we worried about what to do. We searched the landscape in the hope of sighting them. It was impossible to tell, there were soldiers everywhere, all dressed the same, all carrying the same, all walking the same, all looking the same. We tried not to panic. We began to ask the other soldiers around us: 'Any of you seen OC Support Coy.'

'Is he a tall guy? Wears a helmet? Got a gun? Dresses in green camouflage?'

'Yeah, very fuckin' funny. Come on, don't fuck me about. Have you seen the fucker?'

'No. Why? Have you gone and fuckin' lost him?'

'Hey – I'm a fuckin' Private pal, I can't lose no fucker. If I'm lost it's because some cunt's gone and fuckin' lost ME.'

'All right, all right, keep your fuckin' hair on. No, I am sorry, we have not seen the Officer Commanding Support Company. Have you tried our OC? He might know.'

'Where's he?'

'Last seen somewhere over the other side of that ridge (the soldier pointed) apparently doin' his best to earn your mate Blackie and the rest of Company HQ their VCs. Personally, Luke, I wouldn't go within a fuckin' mile of the lunatic. But he's probably your best bet.'

All the soldiers around the speaking man laughed. I also tried to laugh. I failed miserably. We thanked the soldiers for their help and set off over the ridge in search of OC B Coy.

As we reached the top of the ridge I noticed for the first time that there was water to our right. I gathered from the fact that we had earlier passed water to our left that we had cut completely across the battlefield. I then stated the blatantly obvious: 'There's water over there, Bill.'

On the other side of the ridge, in a small valley below, we spotted a group of soldiers, roughly of platoon size, spread out along the ground. We walked down from the top of the ridge and walked towards them. We spotted the OC B Coy. I turned and spoke to Bill:

'Correct me if I'm wrong Bill. But is he wearing a fucking woolly hat?'

He was. Had to admire the man. Here I was wishing I had been issued a flak jacket and another helmet for my helmet and here he was running about with a woolly hat on.

I have seen many glorious visual impressions of the Battle of Goose Green (they mainly depict Colonel Jones's last seconds of existence). In each of them, all of us (the good guys) are depicted wearing our regimental red berets. Believe me, I don't recall any one of us wearing anything but our helmets at any stage of the battle. Except for the OC B Company, Major Crosland. He wore a black woolly hat.

Standing next to the OC B Coy was his clerk, Blackie. I asked him how he was and explained about the loss of our OC: 'Wish mine would fuckin' lose me,' said Blackie.

'No you fucking don't, Blackie. You love me,' said the OC B.

We all laughed.

The OC B was on the radio. I wanted to ask him if he had any idea where my OC was, but he seemed quite busy with the task he had in hand. I can remember being very impressed with his apparent calmness and his control of the things around him. I had the thought that, in some ways, he was lucky to have others to worry about, things to plan. I wished I had. I felt it would help to take my mind off things. Stop me thinking so much. Because the OC B seemed so busy I didn't really fancy interrupting him with a question that I felt would be just an annoyance to him. I turned to Bill and said:

'Go on Bill. You fuckin' ask him.'

'Why me? You fuckin' ask him.'

'You're more senior than I am.'

'No I'm fucking not. We both came through Depot together. How can I be more senior than you?'

'Because you've got two brothers who are corporals, that's how.'

This reasoning didn't wash with Bill. It was left for me to ask. I apologised for interrupting the OC B Coy and asked if he knew where the OC Support Coy was. He said he was sorry, he didn't. He asked if we were OK and then said that, if we wanted to, we were more than welcome to tag along with them. It was up to us.

Typical, the only time I really wanted someone to give me an order, tell me what the fuck to do and they start giving me options.

Eventually, after a little debate, Bill and I decided to keep searching for our OC. We thanked B Coy's Headquarters for their help and they suggested we try over with A company.

'Where's they,' we asked.

'Over that way – somewhere,' they said.

So we went over that way, somewhere, but it wasn't over the rainbow.

Death, polystyrene and me
(Goose Green)

Dear Mother in Heaven . . .

We carried on moving forward. After a while we came upon a position of Argentine trenches that had been cleared by another company from our battalion.

There were no longer any department store dummies – just dead men.

One of the dead moved. Bill and I went over to him, got to our knees and rolled him on to his back. He had been hit in the right side of his head just above the eye.

I know a song that talks about the left side of the brain controlling the right. The right side of this boy's brain lay halfway down his face. As I looked at him his left eye took focus on me. Without really knowing what to do – his cause seemed so lost – I reached for and began to unwrap a shell dressing while Bill took off his helmet in search of his morphine.

Our helmets were lined with white polystyrene in which we had been instructed to cut a hole and tape in our morphine syringe. As I gingerly tried to push pieces of brain back into the hole from which they came, my eye caught sight of the lining in my friend's helmet.

I time flashed . . .

I was a small child again of early junior school age. I remembered that our front room had once had a ceiling made from white polystyrene tiles. One night, while my parents were absent, I found a large cardboard tube in which our new kitchen lino had been packaged and proceeded to bang the end of the tube into the white polystyrene. By doing so I left a large circular dent in each of the tiles. On my parents' return my crime was soon discovered and I was swiftly punished.

I shall never know if our efforts to save the boy would have been in vain. He was soon to die. A sergeant approached and told us to move back. He lifted his machine-gun and fired a burst of bullets into the boy's back. The boy's body moved with the impact of each round.

I felt nothing. We moved on.

The times are many when I think back to the death of the boy with the head wound. Sometimes, in my mind today, I pretend that I jumped up and knocked the gun from the sergeant's hands. I imagine that I picked the boy up and carried him to a First Aid Post. I fantasise that today he still breathes. Because of me.

A few days after the fighting had finished, I sat drunk in a room in Port Stanley in the early hours of the morning with a major. I told the major of the death of the boy with the head wound and how he had come to lose his life, though for some reason I said that it was I who had shot him.

The night of my return to England I once again sat drunk in a room, again in the early hours of the morning, but on this occasion with my sister. I repeated the story of the death of the boy with the head wound and again I said that it was I who had shot him.

I do not know why I told this lie. I have searched my mind many times for understanding and as I write these words I search once more.

Maybe, at the end of the day, the sergeant did the right thing by relieving the boy of his suffering. I do not know. I know this, though; please listen. If you ever feel you must take a man's life, because his cause appears a lost one, try not to shoot him in the back from ten feet. Sit next to him, hold his hand, ask your Lord for understanding and put a bullet through his brain. Though be sure it is the left side because it controls the right.

I often think back to the sights I witnessed that day, usually when I am alone and have put things into my body to ease my pain and to make me sane. To help convince myself that I am still a good man, I ask God to look after the mother of the boy with the head wound. The one-eyed, lying, crying, dying boy. From the Argentine.

Amen.

Laughing, legless, waterskiing dentists
(Goose Green)

Out of nowhere shells began to explode all around me. I dived for cover and once more commenced my inward battle to control my fear and stop my legs from pulling me to my feet and running. To my front, beyond a hedgerow, there was a loud explosion. Through the barrage of noise I heard a scream go out, and then a voice jokingly shouting, 'I've lost my leg. I've lost my leg.'

Then came another voice: 'No you haven't mate. It's over here.'

Someone then pulled the string on a laughing bag they were carrying and we all began to laugh.

Later that day, in another part of another field, during another barrage, I lay next to the soldier with the laughing bag. As each shell exploded he would pull the string on his bag.

During the next lull in the shelling I began to talk to the laughing-bag man and two others from his platoon who lay nearby. I can recall saying something along the lines of they had said fuck-all about this shit down at the careers office and that on my return to England I was going to find the sergeant who had convinced me that the pay was good, I would get most weekends off, and that there was also waterskiing. In fact the sergeant at the careers office had not spoken these words, Billy Connolly once had, but the sergeant did come close.

One of the other soldiers said that he could remember an Army television commercial from his youth and that there was definitely a soldier waterskiing in it.

I was in the Army for nearly five years. I never once saw a waterski and I never met a paratrooper who had.

I think the TV lied.

The laughing-bag man was what would have been described as a senior soldier. He was in his late thirties and yet remained a private. From his equipment he pulled out a piece of leather cloth that was bound in the middle by a leather cord. He undid the knot with his teeth, laid the cloth on the ground and unfolded it. Inside the cloth were two pairs of dental pliers. I asked why he was carrying such things. He replied: 'To acquire gold.'

He was a strange man. He was in a strange place. It was a strange day. He fitted in well.

Open wide please . . .

The child with a rifle
(Goose Green)

The shelling had stopped. We got to our feet and continued to move forward.

I time flashed . . .

I was a child again of maybe five or six years of age. I was in a playground near my house and pushing a swing for a friend. My attention was drawn away from the swing by a passing dog and on its return journey the swing came back and hit me in the eye. I put my hand to my eye and felt blood. The blood began to run down my face and I cried out and ran home. When I reached the house, my mother was in the kitchen. She picked me up, sat me on her lap and began to comfort me.

I returned to Goose Green. More artillery began to land and I dived to the ground.

I time flashed to the future . . .

The war was over and I was dead. I could see myself being buried in the cemetery in Redruth next to my grandfather. I saw all of my family standing around the grave. Alone, at one end of the grave, was my mother. She was crying aloud.

Another shell landed and I returned to the madness around me.

The next morning I lay in a trench with another soldier. The trench had once been occupied by Argentines. One of them lay dead nearby. On the bottom of the trench was a book; I picked it up and was surprised to see that it had been written in English. The book was called *Just William*.

The soldier in the trench with me was called Bill. I

took this to be a bad omen and threw the book away. I could see that Bill was sad. He was staring blankly into the sky and as I looked, his bottom lip began to quiver. I asked what was troubling him. He replied that he was thinking how much his mother would suffer if he was to lose his life. I was not alone.

The next day we searched the bodies of the Argentine dead to identify them and bag up their personal effects. One of the dead possessed some photographs. One of the photographs held a moment in time when he had stood outside a house with someone that we assumed was his mother. We became sad for her and as we passed the photograph between us it made us once again think of our own mothers, back home in England.

I thought about how I was to be the first link in the chain that would carry the news of her son's death to her. The boy's papers said he had been born in 1965. He was seventeen the day he died. The day we killed him.

In Port Stanley, after the killings had stopped, a church service was held for the soldiers of my battalion. At the service the padre asked who had we thought of in that moment of fear; the moment we thought we were going to die.

I thought of my mother.

Before writing the words that you are reading now, I had never written anything longer than a letter. I wrote a song about incidents, a song called 'A Child with a Rifle', and my writings grew from there. Please listen. I will sing the last verse of my song for you:

> It's now ten years later; war's
> memories remain.
> They struggle within him, they still
> cause him pain.
> And the shame that he's feeling,
> it will always remain,

Now his mother is far from his
mind.

Who's a mummy's boy then? All of us, that's who.

If there's no joke, then have a smoke
(Goose Green)

To our front was a reverse slope. Mortar and artillery
shells were still falling around us. I cringed along with
every new explosion. We had been taught that artillery,
because of its projectory, could not hit a reverse slope.
We made towards it. On the slope sat a group of Argentine prisoners. Most of them were wounded, most of them
were crying.

The tears of the wounded prisoners made me nervous.
I wished they'd shut the fuck up, although I could find
no way to judge them for crying.

If life's a piece of shit when you look at it, just for a
while, let go of it, have a good cry – it can help.

We reached the slope, found a piece of empty ground
and lay down on it.

Every now and then a shell flew overhead.

It was very heavy.

On the slope sat a captain of the Royal Marines. I
gathered from watching him that he was a Spanish
speaker. He was interrogating the prisoners. He sat on
the left-hand side of the slope away from the group of
prisoners, who were sat on the right. The Argentine

soldiers he spoke with all looked very young. They also all looked very nervous.

They weren't the only ones.

As I sat watching the Royal Marine interrogator, I worried that I might be about to witness something I had no wish to see. I recalled that in my training we had, off the record so to speak, discussed the use of violence towards prisoners as a means of extracting information. We all agreed that if a prisoner held information, e.g. the location of minefields in ground we had to cover, then we would cut his balls off to find out where they were.

Some people reading this may think differently.

You may even go so far as to judge others who would stoop to such things. You should try not to. If you were in the middle of a war, if you felt true fear, if you knew that you did not want to die, you might suddenly develop an animal urge to know about little things in life like minefields. You might even be able to picture a minefield for what it really is. Little bombs that lie in the ground, little bombs not designed to kill – designed to take legs off. Just like the ones you saw blown off this morning. Fuck, how he screamed.

Please look at your legs now.

I can no longer judge other men. I believe this to be one of the good things that living through a war has put into my soul. If I see on the TV news or read in the papers of soldiers massacring women in Africa, bayoneting children in Croatia, or pushing buttons and putting missiles through bunkers in Baghdad, I find myself feeling sorry for the men who are capable of doing such things. They make me feel sorry for us all.

As I watched the Marine officer interrogate his prisoners I was happy to see that I had no need to worry. I was watching an artist at work. Here's a man that knows what he's about, thought I.

Sometimes he was smiling with the men he interrogated. Other times his face would hold a serious look, he would hold up a finger, wag it to make a point, then say a few lines in Spanish. I never once saw him angry, never once heard him shout and not once did he use violence as a tool to persuade. Though I did on one occasion see him give a cigarette to one of the Argentine prisoners and a light to go with it. This was of course very foolish – smoking can kill.

There were twenty or so other soldiers from my battalion lying on the slope. One of them, a senior NCO, hated me, though I could never figure out why. Not to worry though – the feeling was mutual. He was smoking. I knew he didn't smoke and many times in the past had heard him tell others what a disgusting habit it was. But there he was – smoking.

'Die of cancer, you bastard,' thought I.

It got better. He finished smoking his cigarette and before throwing the butt away, lit a fresh one from it.

I was loving this. He was scared. Go on, please, please, please have another one. I wanted him to. I wanted him to use the butt from his new cigarette to light another with, and then another, and then another. I wanted him to smoke into eternity.

Shells continued to fall and the Argentine prisoners continued to cry. But the shells no longer made me cringe and the tears of the prisoners no longer made me nervous. All of my mind was occupied with the image of the non-smoking man, who hated me, smoking – because he was scared.

His fear took mine away. He bore it for me. I had the thought that I would never fear this man again, I would never take from him the shit I had taken before. Then I had the thought that I would like to go up to him and comment on his smoking. But, I thought, if I did that he might hit me. I didn't want to be hit.

I stayed where I was.

There was a time, in the mind of my past, that I would pretend that I had gone over to him, I liked to imagine that I had said, 'Not smoking are we?' I loved to fantasise that he looked up at me and all I could see was pure undiluted fear.

I always pictured myself laughing in his face.

Today I realise the lie behind my laughter. I am able to remember and face the truth. I too was scared.

I had once fooled myself with a similar thought. It had to do with parachuting. I used to say to myself, as I stood in the door of an aircraft, looking at the distant ground below, awaiting the red light for ready and green light for go, 'Whole world please look at me. I'm a paratrooper and I'm about to jump out of this hundred-mile-an-hour aeroplane into nothing, I'm risking my life just for the kick and I shall never again be scared of anyone or anything.'

This also proved to be a lie.

On our journey home from the Falklands, I lay alone one night in my cabin, half-drunk, half-awake, listening to a conversation that was coming through the walls from the cabin next door. The soldiers in the cabin next door were having a piss-up. Their conversation turned to Hitler and the Holocaust.

A drunken voice, which belonged to a corporal, gave the opinion that Hitler had been right to gas the Jews. He said he hated Jewish fuckers. He then went on to say more, and more, and more. As I listened to the verbal sewage that was seeping from the cabin next door, I found a piece of my mind wanting to watch the loud-mouthed corporal and his family be dragged from their beds at three o'clock in the morning by the Gestapo. I would like to see his face as they stripped him of his clothing and pushed him into an oven.

As he went on and on, I began to feel angry. Very angry. I wanted to get off my bed, go next door and wrap a metal bar straight across his face. But I didn't and I also knew that I never would, because if I did he would kick the shit out of me. It was the fear of this that was the true reason behind my anger.

Today, if I hear such things said, and unfortunately I still do, be it against Jews or gays or blacks or whoever, I no longer wish to resort to violence and I no longer feel angry. I just feel sad.

Who's a little coward then? Ignorant, bigoted shits that's who.

The Gospel according to Luke
(Goose Green)

We were in a gully. I'm not sure how many of us were there. I know I was there, I know Bill was there, there were also three or four soldiers from an anti-tank section plus a few other stragglers. Every few seconds a mortar or artillery round would fly over our heads. I can recall looking skywards, and being surprised at how slowly the shells and rounds appeared to fly through the air. I remember being able to say, 'That's a mortar round,' or 'That's an artillery shell.' I could actually see if the rounds carried fins or not.

With my eyes I followed the rounds to their points of impact. The ground to our rear was marshy bog. The majority of rounds on reaching impact just plopped into the muddy water. If the terrain had not been so soft many more would have lost their lives that day. It was beginning to feel as though I had been under shell-fire all of my life.

I was very scared.

Someone was screaming. As the screams grew louder and louder they occasionally broke into Argentine Spanish and then back again into universally understood screaming. As I lay I tried to block out the screams. I had enough problems without having to listen to that whining wanker. His screams were beginning to annoy me. They were interrupting my thoughts. They were increasing my fear. Someone shouted out: 'I wish that cunt would shut the fuck up, he's doing my fucking head in.'

Once again – I was not alone with my thoughts.

I had had enough. I crawled up the side of the gully and looked over the top. Before me was a plateau of flat ground. The plateau had once held an Argentine defence position – not any more, the ground was now ours. To give proof to this the plateau was under heavy artillery and mortar fire. Heavy Argentine artillery and mortar fire. No more than fifty metres away from me was an Argentine. He was sat down, out of his trench, holding both legs and loudly screaming. I got to my knees and shouted: 'If you don't shut the fuck up, I'll fuckin' shut you up, you cunt.'

At the same time I put my machine-gun to the aim, and pointed it at the wounded Argentine.

I left Goose Green. I left the war. I left myself.

I was overcome with shame. What had I just said? What had I just thought? I didn't mean it. I was scared that's all, just scared.

I turned and looked at the other soldiers in the gully expecting some criticism for my outburst. It didn't come. They said nothing.

Except for Bill. Bill said this: 'Hey, Luke, get a fuckin' grip.'

I got a grip.

'We've got to get the fucker, Bill.'

Another shell landed on the plateau. The Argentine let out another plea.

I wanted to get the screaming man. Bill also wanted to get the screaming man, but we didn't want to leave the gully.

I had an idea.

I told Bill to follow me and we retreated back down the gully towards a group of Argentine prisoners that we had passed earlier on. He was one of theirs – they could go and get him.

We found the Argentines huddled in a row along the side of a reverse slope. I remember looking down on them and being struck by how young they all appeared. Most of them were wounded. Most of them were crying. I kicked the nearest prisoner and gestured with my machine-gun for him to get to his feet.

He started crying aloud. He rolled over on to his knees, put his hands together into the praying position and began to beg at my feet.

Typical, he thought I wanted to take him away and head-job him.

The Argentine would not get to his feet.

The Provo corporal guarding the Argentines turned on us: 'Hey, you two. Fuck off and leave him alone.'

We gave up and ran back up the hill and into the gully. The wounded boy was still screaming.

Well, as my mother used to always say, 'If you want something doing, son, go and do it yourself.'

Bill and I ran up the side of the gully and raced via the most direct route towards the wounded boy. We did not pass go. We did not collect £200. But we did jump over two dead men. I had never jumped over a dead man before. It was the thought I had when I did.

We reached the wounded Argentine. Both his legs were covered in blood. He was still screaming. He noticed our arrival and began to cry loudly just as his prisoner comrade had done a few minutes earlier. He began to beg for his life.

We had no time to listen. There was no time to talk. Shells were still coming in.

Bill and I both grabbed an arm and pulled the still screaming boy back across the position he had lost the use of his legs defending and into the gully.

We reached the gully, and took time to get our breath back and then pulled the boy back down the hill towards the other prisoners. We dropped him next to the one who had earlier refused to come with us. As we were leaving I shouted at the boy who we had just saved, I told him that he was a fucking cunt and then I kicked hard at one of his wounded legs.

You should have heard him scream.

We returned to the gully.

I have often wondered why I kicked the boy. Which is strange because I always knew – others were watching. I may have helped save him but I wasn't soft, I was still hard. See, I just kicked him. I was still a man.

On our return to the gully I can recall lying back down and feeling pride. Pride in me. I knew without thinking that Bill and I had done right.

There are times today, normally at night, just as I lay my head on my pillow, that I look back on my life since that day. I look back on the lies I have told, the times I have stolen. I remember the women I have hurt and cheated on and my crazy moments of uncontrolled rage. I become overwhelmed with shame. I try to stop my mind as it races to look at my past. I desperately try not to think of Kathy, the woman who waited for me through a war and then who waited again, while pregnant, for me to finish a prison sentence. I try not to think of our son. The son I never hold. Because of me.

As my mind falls into despair I try to reach out and grab some piece of good. Something to stop me from falling. My mind finds and rests on the Argentine boy with wounded legs. I recall the overwhelming shame that I felt after threatening him; I remember the over-whelming pride in myself after we had left him with his comrades and returned to the gully.

The memory of the boy with the wounded legs gives me some hope. It helps me find the good in me. The God in me.

Please think now.

Who's dead? He's dead
(Goose Green)

We were still lost, had been for a while. We came across another position of trenches which had once been occu-pied by Argentines. There were no longer any dead men – just department store dummies.

We began to jump from trench to trench looking for things: pistols, night sights, food, whatever. We came across a large green groundsheet.

One of us grabbed a corner and pulled at it to see what it was covering.

It was covering dead men. Some of our dead men.

One of them was Colonel Jones. We couldn't believe it. We didn't want to believe it. We knew the order of things battle-wise and we knew that as he was the Battalion CO he would be at the rear. If he was dead then how many others were also dead? What had happened?

Someone said they must have outflanked us. They

50

must have come up behind and hit our rear. If this was the case then we were in the shit. Deep shit.

We began to search the landscape around us. There were little moving dots of men in the distance in all directions. We wondered if the dots were British or Argentine. We just didn't know.

Today I feel, with what I believe to be shame, that I cannot recall how many others lay motionless with Colonel Jones. It was either two or three. I know Jones was there. I know the adjutant Captain Woods was there. I also know that the second-in-command of A Company, Captain Dent, was there. But I don't recall any others and yet there is a piece of my mind that says there was somebody else – some dead body else who I did not recognise.

I looked at the corpse of Captain Woods and said to the others: 'Fucking hell. Harper's been fucking wasted.'

Harper was a corporal who worked as a battalion Provo. Bill said no, it was Woods. I said no, don't be stupid, it's Harper. Someone else said that it was Woods, look he was wearing his para smock. I looked again at the dead man and noticed the three blue and white cloth pips that lay on his shoulders. They were right, I was wrong – it was Woods.

In the Falklands we had all been issued arctic smocks which bore no rank or other badges that we would normally wear. But Captain Woods was still wearing his para smock. As I looked at his lifeless body I wondered why he had chosen to stick with his para smock and not wear his newly-issued arctic smock like everyone else. I had the thought that he might have done it as a good luck sort of thing.

I had another thought – if this was the case, it hadn't worked.

Captain Woods was the adjutant – we knew that, and Colonel Jones was obviously the Battalion CO – we knew that. But Captain Dent – who was he with? Was he also with the Battalion Headquarters? Or was he with a rifle company? We began to discuss Captain Dent's role within the battalion.

Halfway through the discussion it dawned on me – I knew who he was with. He had once been with us in Support Company and as I was the company clerk I remembered that when he had moved to one of the rifle companies, that company's clerk had called me up to say that Captain Dent's leave record card was missing, and did I still have it? I searched and found that I did and got the company runner to take it over to his new company.

'He's with A Company,' I said.

'Was,' said somebody else.

We all let out a little laugh – but it was a very nervous little laugh.

I once again found myself playing over in my mind times that I had spoken with the dead men who lay at my feet. I remembered Captain Dent sitting on the corner of my desk when he had first joined Support Company. I recalled him telling me about his time with the 21st SAS. He told me that they were known as 'The Artists', which was something I had not known before. I felt sad that I would speak with him no more. He was an exceptionally likeable man, a fair man, a good man. Today, I find that every time I hear mention of the SAS I always catch myself thinking of Captain Dent. I always find myself picturing his lifeless corpse at Goose Green. I always ask myself why a man such as he went any-where near the Army in the first place.

As I looked at Captain Woods I recalled a company piss-up in Northern Ireland at which I had spoken to him for the first time. I heard again his Scottish accent and the way he told me of his great dislike for all things 'Thatcherite'. He told me that he was a socialist and always would be. A socialist officer in the Parachute Regiment was a very rare thing – I had the thought that our regiment would be a worse institution without him.

Colonel Jones was smiling. I saw many dead men on the Falkland Islands but Colonel Jones was the only one that I ever saw who was smiling. As I looked at him I wondered about who or what he was thinking of, as he drew his last breath, that made him in death appear so happy. I remember thinking that I was glad that he appeared to have died a happy man. Someone asked did we know that Colonel Jones was an exceptionally wealthy man. I said I didn't, someone else said that they did and if they were that rich there was no way in the world that they would put 8,000 miles between them and their bank accounts.

We all laughed nervously again.

At the end of the day it turned out that the Argentines had not outflanked us, but that Colonel Jones had stormed to the front when one of the rifle companies had got bogged down and lost their forward momentum.

For this act of heroism/complete insanity (I still can't work it out) he was posthumously awarded the Victoria Cross.

I have read many accounts of the death of Colonel Jones. They range from: charging a trench, getting shot, getting up, recharging another trench and getting shot again, to stepping one pace over the top and getting instantly cut to pieces. I have spoken to many who were there when Colonel Jones lost his life and I have still heard at least three different versions. I was not there so I do not know exactly, or in how brave a way he lost his life. I know this though; please listen.

When Colonel Jones was shot dead at Goose Green he, a half colonel in the Parachute Regiment, who had no business whatsoever putting himself that close to the enemy, was the most forward man of the British Task Forces. That is a fact. Hero or lunatic Colonel Jones was a leader of men.

Whilst still in Port Stanley we read in a British newspaper that the late great Colonel Jones was 'loved' by his men, that we tragically mourned his death, that the memory of our dead colonel – who had laid down his life for us – had driven us to Port Stanley and ensured us of victory.

Bollocks.

We were paratroopers – we loved no one. We had not been taught to love. If one of us died, then no it was not a happy event, but at the end of the day our attitude was one of 'We get paid our money and we take our chances'. Not one of us had been forced to join the Army. We were professional soldiers. We fought for the living not for the dead – the dead were dead.

I know something else. Colonel Jones was also a professional soldier. I cannot believe he would have seen things any differently.

In the same newspapers that we read in Port Stanley we saw for the very first time Colonel Jones being referred to as 'H'. According to the press this was the name we all knew and loved him by.

Bollocks again.

To be fair, and as you already know, I do try to be fair, he was apparently known as 'H' by his fellow officers. But none of us ever hung out in the officers' mess, so 'H' was a new one on us. Reading these untruths made us feel resentful towards the newspapers. It was our facts that they were distorting. We had just fought a war and we believed they had no right to do this to us. No right to wrongly tell the world how we referred to our dead colonel, no right to wrongly tell the world how we felt towards our dead colonel.

Today, if ever I meet or speak on the phone with old comrades from the Falklands War and we talk of Colonel Jones, not once do we refer to him as 'H' – because it was not the name we knew or loved him by. We just call him 'Jones' or 'Jonesie' and we don't love him by it – but believe me, we do respect him by it.

Maggie's insane, organic killer
(Goose Green)

We crossed another field and approached a hedgerow. As we met the hedge we turned left and began to follow it to the corner of the field. A bullet shot past my face. It was so close, I felt it physically. All of us automatically dived to the ground and crawled up to the hedge in search of cover. A voice shouted out: 'Can anyone see the enemy?'

Slowly, one by one, we began to look over the hedge. There was nothing there. Just an empty field and another empty field beyond that. Another shot flew by. Tony screamed and fell to the ground. The two nearest soldiers crawled to where he lay and began to inspect his wound. They called out that he had only been hit in the leg; he would live.

Fear began to push thoughts into my mind. How was it possible? Tony had only his head above the wall at the time the bullet passed. His leg was at least three feet below the bullet's path and it was pressed up against the hedge. How was it possible for him to be hit in the leg? If he could be hit behind the hedge, then so could I. Where would I be hit? In the head? In the chest? A score of impacts rushed through my mind. I became aware that I was working myself up to the edge of panic. I began to try and talk myself into becoming calm. If I was to be hit then I would be hit, that was that and there was nothing I could do about it. I tried desperately to control my thoughts and desperately to steady my breathing.

Someone called out: 'It's a fucking sniper.'

I have some advice for you now, and it's good advice, so try to take it in. If ever you are walking down your local high street and you suddenly come under sniper fire, here's what you do. Try not to panic and dive to the ground. Then look for a phone box and crawl towards it. On reaching the phone box pull down the Yellow Pages and look under 'S' for sniper. Then give one of them a quick call. In other words, you set a thief to catch a thief. There were no phone boxes on the battlefield of Goose Green, but we did have radios. The call was soon made.

We waited a lifetime. Looking back, I realise that it was probably not that long but on the day it seemed like years. Every time one of us moved a shot would fly over the hedge. We were faced with an enemy that we could not even see let alone shoot back at.

We came under mortar fire.

As I lay against the hedge I was willing my body to dissolve into the ground, I could not move, I did not want to move, I also did not wish to remain where I was. I didn't know what I wanted. Except for two things: I knew I wanted the Argentine sniper to die and I knew I wanted the Argentine mortar crew to die. The sooner the better.

As I lay petrified beyond belief, a naive thought entered my mind. I thought that if Margaret Thatcher and her Tory Cabinet were lying where I was, and General Galtieri and his military junta were on the other end of the incoming mortar fire, then this shit would stop instantly.

As I have said this was, of course, a naive thought. Had Margaret Thatcher been at Goose Green she would probably have been right behind Colonel Jones as he stormed the Argentine machine-guns, hitting him with her handbag and telling him to get a move on.

Someone called out: 'If I'd have known I was going to do this much lying down I would have brought a fucking pillow.'

We all laughed. I still laugh at this – it still seems funny.

To our rear I noticed a bush. Not that surprising, we were in a field, but this bush was different – it was moving. I began to have serious doubts about the state of my mental health and so turned to the soldier lying next to me and asked if he could see the bush.

'Do you mean the fucker that's moving?' he replied.

I was okay – the bush was moving. As the bush got nearer to our position it became apparent that it was not a bush but a member of our Sniper Platoon. Snipers like to go around making like bushes, it's part of their job. The bush reached our position and stopped. A shot flew over the hedge, another shell exploded, we all cringed and let out little yelps of fear. The bush stood still, it was as though he had not realised he had just been shot at.

'What's up?' asked the bush.

'What's up? What's fucking up?' came a panic-filled reply. 'I'll tell you what's up, pal. One of your shithead sniper soulmates is using us for fucking target practice, that's what's fucking up.'

Another shot rang out.

'Where is he?' asked the bush.

'Where is he? Where the fuck is he? If I fucking knew that I wouldn't be fuckin' well lying here talking to a cunt like you. I'd be trying to kill the bastard.'

The bush had always held a reputation for being something of a madman and true to form he did not let his reputation down. He jumped up on to the top of the hedge. Two more rapid shots flew over. These were followed by more cringing and yelps on our part but the bush remained still. He obviously had not heard them.

'It's a sniper,' shouted the bush.

'Oh really! Did you hear that boys, it's a fucking sniper! What am I? Am I talking in Czechoslovakian or what? I know it's a sniper, I fuckin' well told you that, now get the fuck off the bastard wall.'

Yet another bullet passed.

'If you don't get off that fuckin' wall, pal, I'll shoot you myself.'

The bush remained on the wall and from under one of his branches he pulled out a pair of binoculars. He put the binoculars to his eyes and slowly began to survey the landscape.

'Definitely a sniper,' declared the bush.

'Why me, why the fuckin' hell is it always cuntin' me? This is your last chance, I won't fuckin' tell you again, get down off that bastard wall.'

'I see him,' said the bush and with that he finally jumped down off the wall and crawled off to our right. After about twenty metres he stopped, aimed his rifle and fired a single shot. He then jumped back on top of the hedge and once more surveyed the landscape with his binoculars.

'Think I got him,' said the bush.

Again, slowly, one by one, we started to look over the hedge. There were no more shots. We began to rejoice; a man had just died and we were happy. Another barrage of mortar fire brought us back to reality.

The soldier who had been hit in the leg had what we would have described as the perfect wound. The bullet had passed clean through his leg without smashing any bones or cutting any major arteries. As we left him with a friend and continued our forward movement he called out that we were to be sure to have a nice day. Then he laughed – we didn't.

I was later told that after the battle the British bush had gone in search of the Argentine bush. On finding his corpse he discovered that he had shot him clean through the head from a distance of over 1,000 metres. The British bush was certainly mentally unbalanced; but he was also certainly a very fine shot. As for the Argentine bush, he is now certainly very dead.

. . . and the angel of the Lord appeared unto him in a flame of fire out of the midst of a bush; and he looked, and behold the bush burned with fire and the bush was not consumed.

Exodus, chapter 3, verse 2

The one I thought would kill me
(Goose Green)

The barrage of shells stopped. It was headless chicken time. Some form of telepathy pulled us to our feet in unison and we ran to somewhere else. Didn't matter where just as long as we got away from this corner of hell on earth. We moved round the reverse slope and into a gully. I noticed that the BBC reporter Robert Fox had joined us.

A shell screamed in.

The world turned to slow motion. In the fraction of a second that it took for the shell to impact I threw myself to the ground and awaited certain pain. Its incoming scream was so loud I knew it was going to land on top of me.

It impacted.

The earth shook, noise ripped through my brain, my ears rung in pain, soil fell from the sky. I held hands with my mother, lay naked with my wife.

Then – I was still alive. I lifted my head from the ground and looked at the men around me. They all looked alike, their faces all held the same question: 'Am I really still alive?' I turned my head to the right, the ground was smoking. Not more than a foot away from where I lay ran an almost perfectly straight line of smoking, copper-coloured shrapnel.

In my own mind, I have two versions of what happened next and it's strange, because today, ten years on, with the war long gone, I believe in the second version which up until a few months ago I had strongly denied.

This is the first version: I picked up a piece of the smoking, copper-coloured shrapnel and passed it to the BBC man, Robert Fox, who was lying next to me. I was wearing gloves and so did not feel the heat of the shrapnel. As Robert Fox, with fingers bare, took the shrapnel from my hand its heat immediately forced him to drop it.

The other version of events is that it was Robert Fox who passed the shrapnel to me and it was I who had dropped it.

At RAF Brize Norton, on the day we returned from the Falklands, I noticed Robert Fox standing in the airport lounge. As I looked at him I thought, 'That's a nice suit he's wearing, shame it's two sizes too big.' We had all lost weight on the Falklands. He had a tie around his waist keeping his trousers up. I walked up to him and asked if he remembered me and also did he remember 'that shell'. He said he did remember me and that he would also always remember 'that shell'.

A few months later Robert Fox's book on the Falklands War was published. I was not a happy little trooper. Firstly, there was a photograph of our company head-quarters which had been taken on Sussex Mountain and you could only see the top of my head. Not to worry, I thought, he's bound to have mentioned that shell and me passing him the shrapnel. He had. Well, mentioned the shell. But there was no mention of me. Instead he said that someone else, who I presumed was a hat because I had never heard of him, had passed it to him.

As I said, today I am not so sure that it was I who had passed him the shrapnel. At RAF Brize Norton, only a few weeks after the event, I was very sure.

While writing these words my memories have continued to pull from my mind more memories. The more I write – the more I recall. I close my eyes and in the same way that I would watch a movie, I watch again my past. Today, when I close my eyes and remember the shell that I thought would kill me I see the BBC reporter, Robert Fox, lying next to me. He's dressed in camouflage clothing just like me but he doesn't have a gun. I see him hold out an open hand. Lying in the hand is a piece of copper-coloured shrapnel. It's smoking. I take the shrapnel from his hand. I immediately drop it. It's hot.

If I ever meet Robert Fox again I shall ask him what he sees when he closes his eyes.

Despite being able to visualise and watch again in detail the shell that I thought would kill me I have only once truly remembered it. Remembered the true feeling, the true fear.

I was thinking of Goose Green. I remembered the shell again.

The memory exploded in my mind.

For a flash, I felt again how I felt as I lay waiting for pain. I heard again the shell screaming in. I heard it explode. Felt the earth shake, soil fall on my back.

I let out a short high-pitched yelp of fear and jumped to my feet. The real memory vanished. The true remembrance of fear passed, leaving me with a new fear. I had the thought that I had gained some knowledge of madness. I then inhaled the smoke from some burning herbs.

Who's scared and mad? Probably me and probably you – that's who.

'Boo.'

Figments of my imagination?
(Goose Green)

We were being shelled. I was once again wishing I could dissolve into the ground. There was no nothing any more. Just shells coming in and my fear going out. I had never before been so scared. I had never before prayed so hard, promised so much. I looked up from the ground and over to my left.

I saw something unbelievable.

I saw my Aunt Letty. Aunt Letty was not really an aunt, but the second wife of my grandfather on my mother's side. To me she was the only grandmother I knew. She had been dead for seven years. I don't know how far away she was. I don't know what she was wearing. I don't remember anything about her, except that she was there. She was definitely there.

There on the battlefield of Goose Green.

She was smiling at me and at the same time, with her hands, she was calling for me to come to her. I got to my feet and ran towards her. As I reached the point where she had been standing, a shell came screeching in behind me. I dived to the ground. There was a loud explosion, the noise ripped into my mind, I covered my ears to try and stop the painful ringing. I lifted my head from the ground. Aunt Letty was no longer there. I looked behind, to where the shell had impacted. It had landed on the exact spot I had occupied before Aunt Letty had waved me to move.

On the night of my return to England, the night that I sat drunk in the early hours of the morning with my sister Micky, the night I spoke of the death of the boy with the head wound, I told of how I had seen our Aunt Letty on the battlefield of Goose Green. I told Micky how I would not be talking to her now if I had not seen her. I asked my sister to believe me. Micky said she did. She told me that as news of our advance to Goose Green was announced she had gone into her garden. She said it was a bright night. The sky was filled with stars. She said she looked up to the heavens and quietly asked Aunt Letty to watch over me. To please try and help bring her little brother back alive to her.

Her calls were answered.

One day I shall thank Aunt Letty. It's one of the few certainties I have.

Screaming, dreaming and embarrassed
(Goose Green)

We saw aerials rising above a hedgerow in a corner of the field. We moved towards them. We reached the hedge and jumped over. We saw Jed. Thank fuck. We were lost no more.

The OC wasn't with Jed. I don't know why. I'm sure I asked and I'm sure Jed replied. But I can't remember the reply. Didn't matter, we were no longer alone. We were in Radio City.

That's what I've always called it. Radio City. Every man and his dog seemed to be there. They all had radios and the radios all had aerials. Aerials that reached into the sky, that poked above the hedge to our front. They were soon noticed.

We came under mortar fire.

I had no need to hit the deck. I was already there. I had already learned; if you're not doing anything – then lie down. It can save your life.

The shelling increased, I could hear in the distance the sound of approaching jets. We were told they were Harriers. As the jets flew directly overhead the day exploded into sound.

Once again everything turned to slow motion. I felt a sharp pain in my back. It hurt so much that it didn't. I was lifted into the air; I felt as though I was hovering. I screamed aloud: 'I've been hit. I've been hit.'

I fell to the ground and reached my hand behind my back. I found myself breathing heavily. My back felt very warm. I was convinced I was bleeding. I twisted my head to look over my shoulder, I could see smoke rising from my back. I found my mind pulling itself back from complete panic. In seconds I told myself that I was still breathing, that my heart was still beating, that I would live.

I time flashed to the future . . .

I was in a bed with white sheets. The bed was on a hospital ship. I could see a nurse.

I returned to Goose Green. I said to myself, 'Just get me the fuck out of here.'

Someone was holding my hand. I could hear two voices saying, 'It's all right Luke, it's all right.' It was Jed and the Mortar Officer, Captain Tonks. Jed rolled me over on to my stomach. Suddenly he pulled me back around on to my back. In his hand he held a small metal disc. He said it was this that had hit me. Then he hit me – but not very hard. My screams had scared the shit out of all around me.

The small metal disc had once been part of a Blowpipe missile. On hitting me it had cut through my back webbing strap plus five layers of clothing and left me with a small nick that it would have been over the top to have put a plaster on.

After the battle, and even to this day, the piss was taken out of me severely for my screams of, 'I've been hit. I've been hit.' At one time I did try to explain just how frightening that moment had been for me, but soon gave this up for a lost cause.

I read in another book that when I was caught in the Blowpipe's back blast I ran around screaming, 'I've been hit, I've been hit.' This is not true. I did not run around. But I did scream.

Later, in Goose Green, Captain Tonks tried to console me when the boys were taking the piss. He said he was happy the bloody thing hadn't hit him, he wouldn't have known what to do. His words cheered me up. Another officer, Captain Ketley of the Anti-Tanks, was also caught in the back-blast. He told me that the metal disc had missed his face by inches as it flew by. He said he dreaded to think what it would have done to his face if it had hit him. This also made me feel better.

Much later, in Aldershot, I began to think about what went through my mind when I thought I had been hit. I felt shame that my first thought on realising that I would live, was to get the fuck out of Goose Green and get aboard a hospital ship. In the war movies I had seen, an injured soldier had always wanted to stay on the battle-field with his comrades.

Today I no longer feel shame for this thought. I now realise it was very human.

Yesterday, I spoke with Steven Hughes, who had been our medical officer during the Falklands campaign. I retold the story of being hit by the backblast and the thoughts that ran through my mind immediately after-wards. I told him that I had checked that I was still breathing, that my heart was still beating and that my body was not bleeding. He replied that he was

very pleased to hear this. He said that obviously his
weeks of drilling battle casualty procedure into us had
worked. Check airways, check bleeding – that's what he
taught.

Without a doubt he taught us well.

Worrying dead litter bugs
(Goose Green)

We had reached the point where we could look down on
to the settlement of Goose Green. For the first time, we
held high ground above the enemy. We knew the advan-
tage had swung to us. The noises of war began to fade
into a very silent silence, darkness began to draw over
the battlefield.

There was talk that a ceasefire had been called. This
was good news, we might now get out of this alive. I
asked if anyone knew why a ceasefire had been called?
Had we asked for it or had they?

'Didn't they tell you, Luke? The Argy conscripts have
to be in bed by eight. So we've promised not to attack
them again until after they've had their little morning
lie-in and eaten up their breakfasts.'

From what I had seen of the Argentine conscripts, I
could have almost believed that.

I was with the OC and Jed. Between us we dug in. I
couldn't call what we dug a trench, it was just a deep
hole. Something for us to sleep in, something to get below
ground level in should the shelling start again.

I looked out from our hole and noticed a major from one of the rifle companies. He was stood amongst a group of soldiers, passing down information and giving orders. Another soldier, who was standing nearby, took from his equipment a packet of sweets – Spangles to be exact. He took a Spangle from the packet, unwrapped the paper around it with his teeth, spat the paper on to the ground and then began to suck on his sweet. The rifle company major noticed this. He flipped his lid.

He shouted at the soldier to pick the wrapper up. He said we might be at war but that was no excuse for us to let our discipline drop.

The soldier apologised and picked the wrapper up.

The major's outburst brought a few astonished looks from the surrounding men (especially from the ones behind him), me included. It did seem a touch ridiculous that here we were in a field full of dead men, expended ammunition cases everywhere, fire burning away very nicely along the hedgerow ten feet away, and the major's losing his head over a sweetie wrapper.

'The cunt will have us out area cleaning in the morning.'

I tried not to laugh too loudly.

If we had taken the time to think, we would probably have realised that he was absolutely correct in having a go at the litter-bug soldier. If any of us was ever to drop rubbish whilst on exercise in England we would have had our balls ripped off. To drop rubbish is an undisciplined thing to do. If others should find it, it can tell them an awful lot about you, i.e. in this case it's a Spangle wrapper, therefore British soldiers have been here.

On the other hand, it's probably fair to argue that the dead Argentines lying around, littering the ground, might also be a bit of a giveaway as to our presence. A dead giveaway.

As darkness pushed over the horizon and the light

finally vanished from the battlefield I settled into the bottom of our hole. It was cold. During the day I had sweated quite a lot, and the sweat had left a fine layer of moisture on my body which was trapped by my clothing. I remember wishing that I had my bergen. I had a sleeping bag in my bergen. I had more food, a change of clothes. I told myself tough shit you haven't got it, so stop whining on about it.

Then I did some more thinking.

I reviewed the day's events, hoping to come to some sort of conclusion. The killed, the killing, the fear, the laughter, even the tears. I tried to understand something. Tried to convince myself that I had learned something.

What had I learned? I had no wish to die – that's what I had learned.

My mind kept replaying fragments of time from the day. I saw and heard again the shell that I thought would kill me. For a fraction of a second I felt again the intense fear. I chilled. Then my mind made me watch once more the shell that I thought would kill me. Once more it didn't kill me, but it did take my leg off. I chilled some more.

I began to tell myself that the shell had not killed me, it had also not taken my leg off. I said, 'It never has and it never will. Why worry, Ken? All's well that ends well.'

I then had trouble convincing myself that lying in a hole, with an enemy lying in another hole a few hundred yards away, was a very 'well' type ending.

Me worry? I tried to tell myself. Let him fucking worry. He's the one that's really got something to fucking worry about.

Eventually, tucked between a man called Hugh Jenner and another man called Jed Peatfield, exhaustion took over my mind and I fell into sleep.

But just before I fell into sleep I said my prayers.

I said, 'Thank you. Amen.'

I eat, I shit, I am (2)

The next major moment in my Falklands tale of eating and shitting happened at Goose Green during the night after the day's fighting. I had fallen asleep in a hole that I had dug with the OC and Jed, but the cold of the night had prodded me awake. I got up from our hole and decided to go walkabout in an attempt to warm up. Only a few yards from our hole a hedgerow of gorse burned brightly against the backdrop of the night. The fire had been caused by shells of some type hitting the ground around the gorse and setting alight the peat below. As the day had gone on and turned into night, the fire had progressed, and eventually the peat began to glow with heat. Around the glowing ground sat many soldiers, most of whom had taken off their boots and were drying them and their feet in the warmth. I walked towards the glow, found a space and sat down. It was heaven. So warm. I lay back and stretched full out along the ground. It warmed the whole of my body. I wanted to stay there for the rest of my life.

Every so often a voice could be heard shouting out, 'Oh fuck!' followed by the noise of the swearing soldier attempting to stamp out the piece of his clothing or equipment that had caught fire because it had been pressing against the ground for too long.

At some point a sergeant who was sitting next to me passed me a mess tin with a spoon in it. In the mess tin was a portion of oatmeal from an Arctic ration pack mixed with a drinking chocolate sachet. He told me I could have two spoonfuls. I was actually starving hungry, but it wasn't until I ate my first spoonful of chocolate oats that I realised it. I had forgotten about eating. I think this was because recently I had been spending so much time thinking about breathing. I can say this now, hand on heart, honest to God and hope to catch the clap if I'm lying, that the chocolate oats that I ate that night upon the battlefield of Goose Green were without doubt the most delicious food I have ever had the pleasure of putting into my body.

Who's alive? We're alive. Happy Days
(Goose Green)

I stood on a beach. It was warm, beautiful and bright. The water was clear blue, the sand below snow white and my skin was tanned a reddish brown. In one of my hands I held a very tall glass, the very tall glass held a very cool drink. Others were there, a yellow bikini, tanned breasts, gentle laughter. Very warm. Very happy.

Someone woke me from my sleep.

'Shit.'

Shit, shit, shit, shit, shit. I was back at Goose Green. I became very cold. Very unhappy. I wanted back to the beach – it was warm, there were drinks. Women.

It was still dark. We had to move before daybreak. We once again found ourselves with the machine-gun platoon. We were to move a short distance over the hedgerow to our front, into a position of trenches that had once been occupied by Argentines. From these trenches we would have a clear field of fire down on to the settlement of Goose Green.

For the second time in as many days we were going to get things going.

It didn't take long to get into order, move quietly forward, jump over the hedge, move forward some more, find our new place, move into the new trenches. We were told to keep our heads down, avoid being spotted by the Argentines below.

The trenches were hurriedly dug shell scrapes no more than two feet deep. To keep out of sight Bill and I lay down, feet to head, head to feet. Daylight broke and we got our first view of the settlement below – we also got our first view of a dead Argentine who lay a few yards away. Shit we were close. I wished it was night again.

Bill and I began to talk. I commented to Bill how none of the dead bodies I had so far encountered had smelled. I had always believed that dead people smelled. Bill thought that the reason none of them smelled was because it was so cold. As we talked about yesterday, we worried about what the day before us would hold. We hoped it wouldn't turn out to be a day like yesterday. We knew that the attack on the settlement below would be started by the machine-guns of our position. We also knew that the Argentines would then throw everything they had at the ground we lay upon to stop the suppressing fire. This was knowledge we could do without.

The day before, Bill and I had been roughly in line with the trench that we were now in, only a few hundred yards over to the right. While there, an Argentine anti-aircraft gun had been put into the 'ground-roll' and fired at us. The resulting shells exploded in mid-air, leaving little white puffs of smoke.

The little white puffs of smoke were a new one on me. On seeing them for the first time I wondered what type of weapon was causing them. I gathered that they were deadly and it worried me that I didn't know from what weapon they came. Did they have something we didn't? And what was the best thing to do when it was fired at you?

If the little white puffs of yesterday could reach where they did, then today, they would reach where we were. We wished our trench had some overhead cover.

We heard someone shouting to our left. It was Jed. He was going mental with someone. Bill and I lifted ourselves up a little and peeked over the left-hand side of our hole. We wanted to see who was on the receiving end of Jed's outburst.

It was some of the Munchkins (the Munchkins being our nickname for the Machine-Gun Platoon). At the time there was a television commercial being shown at home for Jaffa Cake biscuits. It was a cartoon whose stars were little men who ate nothing but Jaffa Cakes: the Munchkins. At some point a few of the Machine-Gun Platoon had been spotted scoffing a pile of Jaffa Cakes. Someone had said, 'Look at the Munchkins' – the name stuck.

The reason Jed was doing his nut was because a few of the Munchkins were out of their trenches, walking around, having a nice chat and passing round the Jaffa Cakes as if they were on a military picnic.

If the Argentines didn't know we were here before – they knew now. Bill and I slid back down to the bottom of our trench and wished we were somewhere else.

Time passed slowly, then a message was shouted for all to hear. The shouts informed us that two Argentine prisoners would be walking through our position and down into the settlement. They were taking a surrender ultimatum to the Argentine commander. The shouts then ordered us not to open fire.

The two Argentines appeared over the hedge to our rear, they walked past our position and into the settlement. I silently wished them luck.

More time passed, once again slowly, then a message was shouted that the Argies were jacking. Bill and I both smiled and laughed, then smiled some more, then laughed, then we shook hands, then we smiled again, laughed again, smiled some more and then did it all over again.

The soldiers of the other trenches that made up our position were now all out of their holes. They were also all smiling. They were also all laughing. A radio operator shouted out that the Argentines wanted to parade and sing their National Anthem before they surrendered. I said to Bill that I'd go and fucking sing it with them, if it would help them to surrender.

We both laughed again. Really hard and really loud.

Bill and I climbed from our hole and went over to Major Jenner and Jed's trench, where everyone else was gathering. Everyone was happy. Everyone was smiling.

And why the fuck not? We were alive and more to the point it was looking like we had a chance to stay that way.

More time passed, then we were ordered via the radio to move down into the settlement. We got our kit together and set off to cover the last few hundred yards into Goose Green. We hit a track and followed it down. As we neared the first buildings of the settlement, the Argentine prisoners began to come into view. There were lots of them. Lots and lots of them.

I don't recall if at the time I had an idea of how many Argentines there were facing us at Goose Green. I think I thought about a battalion. It turned out that there were three times that amount. I remember on seeing them for the first time how many of them seemed to be of Indian extraction and how well fed and clothed they all appeared. They also all appeared to be something else: happy. They all looked very happy.

And why the fuck not? They were also alive and it was looking like they too had a chance to stay that way.

As we approached the settlement we were all still wearing our helmets. I shouted to the OC, asking if we could put our berets on. He either didn't hear me or ignored me – so I asked again. This time he stopped us, we took off our helmets, and we put on our red berets.

It was Conquering Hero Para time.

Civilians ran out to meet us, they applauded as we passed. Young girls ran up to us. We kissed the girls, but none of them cried. Children wanted our autographs, grown men asked to shake our hands. It was a moment of great pride.

As we celebrated our victory a TV news crew arrived and began to film. Dave took a Union Jack from his equipment, he climbed up the side of a building, got on to the roof and hoisted his flag up a pole. Everyone cheered, the TV people filmed.

I was filmed that day in Goose Green. I was drinking Bacardi rum straight from the bottle at the time. When we returned to England and I watched videos of the war I was very pleased to see my own image. Everyone agreed that I looked very warrie.

It is a strange thing for me to have, moving pictures of myself at war. I have watched the footage many times. Sometimes it makes me sad, other times happy. But whether happy or sad, I always end up feeling confused. There's a bit of me that feels I should understand something now, though I don't know what. I always try very hard to experience again the complete happiness that I felt on that morning in May, though I always fail.

Not long after being filmed, I was sent by the OC to find the Argentine military doctor. I stopped a local woman and asked her if she knew where their medical centre was. She said she did and if I followed her she would take me there. As we walked she began to talk about the Argentine doctor. She said he was a fine man who had done everything within his power to help the civilians of Goose Green and if at all possible would we please not shoot him. I said we had no intention of shooting any of them and certainly not the doctor. After the treatment that the inhabitants of Goose Green had received at the hands of the Argentines it is maybe not too surprising that a few of them expected some form of revenge.

Once I had found the doctor, who turned out to be one of those rare human beings that you find yourself liking within the first few minutes of meeting them, I passed on my officer's request and departed.

Then, with a few others, I walked around the houses of the settlement. All the ones that I saw had been very badly vandalised. They also all had piles of human shit in every room. Most of the shit was on the floor, though there was some on beds, chairs and even in the sink in one house. The shitting habits of the Argentines was the only thing that I could not understand. Why shit on someone's bed? On their furniture?

I think that if I came home one day to a house full of shit, I just might like to line the culprits up against a wall and shoot them.

Though I'd make them clean it up first.

German soldiers in leather boots
(Goose Green)

Our first night in Goose Green after the battle was spent in a garage. There were seven of us there and the mood was good.

I had my photograph taken in the garage that night and should these words ever be published I would like the photograph to be printed alongside. Underneath it, I would write these words : 'Me in the garage in Goose

Green that night'. We were drinking tea, smoking cigarettes and listening to our previous day's exploits via the BBC World Service on an old radio that we had acquired from an empty house.

A soldier entered the garage carrying a pile of boots he had taken from the Argentine dead. He found an empty space on the floor, sat down and began to try the boots on. Their boots were of far better quality than ours and as he discarded pairs, others picked them up and also began to try them on.

I time flashed . . .

I was a child again. It was a rainy Sunday afternoon and I was watching an old black and white film on the television. The film told the story of a group of German school-friends, who had left their education to go and fight for the Fatherland in the trenches of the First World War. Later, I was to read the book on which the film had been based – *All Quiet on the Western Front.* I remembered that in the film one of the soldiers, who came from a wealthy family, had been bought a soft pair of leather boots. All of his comrades were envious of his boots and when he was later killed one of them took them from his corpse and began to wear them. In turn, the new owner of the boots was also killed and someone else then took the boots from his corpse.

I returned to the garage in Goose Green and it seemed as though the conversation around me was being spoken in German. I did not touch the Argentine boots.

Later, near Port Stanley, I came across the body of a dead British soldier. He was wearing Argentine boots. I thought that he had probably not seen the film I had watched on that rainy Sunday afternoon many, many years before.

I know another song. It goes like this: 'These boots are made for walking and that's just what they'll do, and one of these days these boots are going to walk all over you.'

Nancy was not lying.

I've got myself six prisoners
(Goose Green)

The latest Really Brilliant, Rule Britannia, God Bless Our Gracious Queen news is that they've put us in the shop at Goose Green. God bless their little shoulder pips.

I love a good lootin'.

The first time we entered the shop there were four or five of us. There was mess everywhere. Shelves were tipped over. Products lay scattered on the floor. I can remember walking amongst the shelves and feeling that I should take something. Almost as if it was my duty to. The first thing all of us did was look for batteries of Walkman size. Even if we didn't have Walkmans, batteries for them would be a useful commodity, something we could barter with. Number two on the list was film, preferably 110 colour. I didn't have a camera but I knew a man who did.

As we passed from shelf to shelf a captain of the Royal Marines entered the shop. He noticed us walking between the shelves and said something along the lines of, we shouldn't take anything, we were highly-trained, disciplined soldiers and if he was to see any of us looting he would personally report us to our colonel.

Someone asked if he'd like a hand to dig him up. We all laughed.

The marine captain did not hear the comment, and so questioned what was so funny. No one answered. We just blanked him. He gave us one more warning and left.

I remember it being a strange experience, the Royal Marine captain coming into the shop at Goose Green. I had the thought, when he spoke, that he had no right to give us orders. Who the fuck did he think he was? We were paratroopers. We had just fought a glorious battle. He was a marine. We hated marines. How dare he even think about fucking talking to us? I decided to just ignore him. Today I find this strange, because the marine officer in question had been with us all the way through the battle of Goose Green. He had faced the same threat as us, witnessed the same killing and probably even experienced the same amount of fear. He had more than a right to speak to us – he had a duty. At the end of the day he was almost one of us. But not quite. He wore a green hat and we wore red ones.

As I said, being put in the shop was really good news, and as with any really good news, it came hand in hand with some really bad news.

The really bad news is that the shop's in a right state, there's shit everywhere (literally) and I don't outrank no one.

'Clean it up, Luke,' said company sergeant-major Jed Peatfield.

'Roll on the day I zip up your body bag,' thought I.

Next scene in the war movie starring me, I'm holding a brush, sweeping the shop floor and happily picturing sweeping up bits of Jed. Of course, I had no wish to really sweep up blown-off pieces of Jed, he was a very likeable man. It was the order I didn't go a lot on.

Enter stage right: Colour-Sergeant Frank Pye.

'What the fuck are you doing, you stupid cunt?' said Frank.

'If I told you I was sweeping the floor, Colour, would you believe me?'

'Don't get fucking gobbie with me, you crow, or I'll fucking drop you.'

'Sorry, Colour.'

Frank went on to explain that his addressing of me as a stupid cunt was not just one of his little terms of endearment, it had some very sound reasoning behind it.

Why was I cleaning the shop when there were 1,200 plus slaves at my disposal up in the prison shed? Why they didn't make the likes of Frank Pye into automatic generals was beyond me. The man's a genius, I thought.

I thanked Frank for his advice and departed the shop in search of my work party. The prisoners at Goose Green were kept at the top end of the settlement in a large sheep shed. The fact that there were over 1,200 of them in the one building should give you some idea of how large the shed was.

On entering the prison shed the first thing I noticed was an old man. He was wrapped in a blanket and looking as though the effort he was using just to stand would be the death of him. I've seen a few pathetic humans in my time but the old man in the prison shed at Goose Green was without doubt the worst. I couldn't work out what someone of his years was doing there.

As I looked at him he began to be surrounded by what appeared to be the complete Argentine Officer Corps. I asked the nearest British soldier what was going on. He explained that death on two legs in the blanket was the Argentine military padre and all of the officers were getting together because they were all about to go outside and hold a Prayer Meet so that the last rites could be administered to the Argentine dead.

'Fair enough,' thought I.

I asked the soldier if he knew how I went about signing out a few prisoners for a work party. He pointed me to a corner of the shed where a group of battalion Provo staff plus a few others were standing around a desk.

One of the soldiers, whose name was Don, was a good friend of mine. We had shared a room together in Northern Ireland and he had been the best man on the day Kathy and I married. I knew him and his sense of humour well: he was a devout Pythonist. I walked over to him and fed my opening line:

'I wish to see the officer in charge – I 'ave a complaint.'

'A complaint? About what?'

'It's about this Argentinian that I signed out from this very shed only this morning. He's dead.'

'Dead. No, he's not dead. He's sleeping.'

(Rest of Parrot sketch, etc.)

Our little piece of acting brought a large amount of applause and laughter from the British contingent and looks that said, 'See, they are all fucking mad,' from the surrounding Argentines.

I explained to one of the Provo staff that I needed a few bodies to help clean up the shop and assured him I had the authority of no less a person than Margaret Thatcher herself. He asked how many I wanted. I said I didn't know. How many was everybody else taking? He said they liked to sign them out in sixes. Would that do? I said six would be fine – thank you very much. One of the other Provos called over an Argentine officer who spoke English and the request for men was passed on. The Argentine officer nodded agreement, turned and spoke a command in Spanish to another Argentine who then disappeared into the crowd of prisoners behind him.

Whilst waiting for the arrival of my six prisoners, I noticed an Argentine soldier sitting cross-legged on the floor behind the Provos' desk. On the floor in front of him were two opened British Army ration packs, a British Hexam cooker, on which food was cooking in a British mess tin, a packet of duty-free Players No. 6 King Size cigarettes and a box of British matches. In one of the soldier's hands was half a packet of Rolos and from the muching sounds he was making, I presumed that in his mouth was the other half.

I turned to the Provo and asked who he was and why he appeared to be getting such preferential treatment.

'Oh him,' said the Provo. 'That's our Manuel, as we like to call him. Found him this morning at the back of shed. He's one of us, Luke. He's a Argy paratrooper. Terrific bloke he is. Says that there's a load of Argy marines in Port Stanley and if we would care to re-arm him, he'd be only too happy to have a go at them with us. Did you know they jumped out of Hercs as well?'

'No, I can't say I did. I hope you invited him to join us in Port Stanley when we have a go at our marines.' Everyone laughed, Manuel included.

'I fookin hate the hats,' said Manuel in broken English.

Obviously the Provo staff had been teaching him important phrases from the British paratroopers' handbook.

I turned away from the Provo and Manuel and started to talk to the English-speaking Argentine officer. He was a large man, very stocky with a small black moustache and immaculately dressed for someone who had supposedly just given his all for the Fatherland. He wore a green beret. I asked him what unit he belonged to. He said he belonged to an élite Argentine commando unit. As we talked it would be fair to say that he began to look down on me. He obviously thought I was beneath him. He was an officer – I was a private. This was his mistake.

I thought back to the dead bodies of yesterday. I thought back to the dead bodies I had just walked past, lined up against the hedgerow outside. The bodies all had two things in common. All of them were Argentines and none of them were officers.

We had lost seventeen men the day before, five of them were officers.

I had seen more dead Argentines than I could count, but I could count the dead officers amongst them. Nil.

These statistics told me a lot about the immaculately dressed, green-hatted hero who stood in front of me now.

I consciously made the decision to show him just exactly who was above who in the little play that we found ourselves destined to act out. If life's a piece of shit when you look at it – take it out on someone else. It can help.

I ripped the beret from his head, hoping that the humiliation of having his regimental honour shat upon would drive him to jump on me, and thereby win for himself a really good kicking from the rest of the British soldiers around me.

Didn't work – he just smiled. Inside the beret was a live bullet sewn into the lining. I asked the officer what the bullet was for. He said it was for honour. Should they run out of ammunition then the bullet in the beret was for them to take their own life with rather than face the dishonour of being captured.

I laughed so hard, I nearly died.

I called over to Don and the Provos and told them the one about the bullet in the beret. Don asked the Argentine officer would he please mind explaining why it was then that we had over a hundred of his green-hatted wankers in the shed with us now. We all laughed. The Argentine officer didn't.

Eventually the Argentine who had been dispatched earlier returned with my six prisoners in tow. They consisted of five army conscripts and another one of the commissioned 'Hero Sons of the Malvinas'.

I turned to one of the Provos and asked, 'What's the score with these then?'

'You have to sign for them here,' he produced a writing pad and I signed, 'the officer don't work and can we please have them back by five?'

The Argentine officer walked over, wagged his finger in my face, and said, 'I no work.'

I asked the Provo if I had to bring him back. The Provo said I did, I had signed for him. Of course if I wanted to sign him back in and then take him away and not bring him back then that would be okay. Just so long as the paperwork was correct. He liked to keep correct paperwork.

Everyone laughed really loudly – except the Argentine officer – he looked really worried. I thanked the Provo for his help, said goodbye to Don and called my six prisoners to attention. Then I shouted at them, 'As you were.' Which was a complete waste of time as none of them, except the officer, spoke English, and he for some reason seemed to have developed a complete downer towards me.

Fuck him – I had the gun.

I snapped to attention, as a demonstration of what I wanted. The five Argentine conscripts all let out little ahs and smiles of understanding and then snapped to attention. Well sort of – it was more like falling asleep into the attention position. But they got there. Then I shouted, 'Squad right.' This brought panic into the eyes of the conscripts. What had he, the one with the gun, just said? They were obviously in the attention position, so chances were I wanted them to turn. But which way? I nodded my head to my right, they all smiled again and then turned to their left.

I was loving this.

I marched them out of the shed and towards the shop. On the way we passed a row of their dead comrades. I asked the officer if he was having a nice day. He said he wasn't.

Along the way I composed a song. It sums up very well how I felt about walking around with six men on the end of my machine-gun:

> I've got myself six pris-o-ners
> and all of them are mine
> you see I have a ma-chine-gun
> it's that that makes them mine.
>
> I love to walk around with them
> so everyone can see
> That Kenny's got six pris-o-ners
> and they're not getting free.

OK, I know it's not chart-topping stuff, but it's honest.

We reached the shop, I pointed to the mess and the prisoners got on with it. The officer spoke a little broken English and I began to talk with him. From what I could make out he had been in the Army since he was six. His father had been a military man and he had followed in the family tradition. He also talked about Port Stanley and the amount of men that they had there. He said there was no way that we would ever capture Port Stanley. I said he was wrong.

After a few hours of work I decided to give my prisoners a little tea break. I got my cooker out of my webbing and brewed them some water. When the drinks were made I stopped the prisoners working and told then to have a rest.

While the seven of us sat around the shop drinking tea, smoking cigarettes and eating biscuits courtesy of the shop, the Regimental Sergeant-Major entered the room with a small group of Falkland Islanders in tow. He took one look at my little tea party and went fucking berserk. He asked what the fuck I thought I was doing. I explained that the prisoners had been cleaning the shop and that I had given them a break.

He said that if they needed a break I should take the fuckers outside and lie them face down in the mud. The ferocity of the RSM's outburst seemed totally out of character. I felt like saying so and also defending my decision to give the prisoners a rest, but he was the RSM and I would sooner tell Rear-Admiral Sandy Woodward to go and get fucked than cross swords with him.

I immediately jumped to my feet and began shouting at the prisoners to return to work. The RSM and the Islanders had a quick walk around the shop and then left. As they were going out of the door the RSM turned to me and, behind the backs of the Falkland Islanders, winked and nodded his head in their direction.

I was greatly relieved. Now I understood. The RSM

had had a go at me for the benefit of the Islanders, the majority of whom believed we should take the Argentines outside and execute the lot of them. The Islanders of Goose Green had had their houses taken over and ransacked and had also spent the last month all locked up together in the Community Centre. Of all the Falkland Islanders, the inhabitants of Goose Green had suffered the most hardship at the hands of the Argentines. It should be no surprise that they held little sympathy for their former captors.

When my prisoners had finished their task and the shop was clean I picked up some British cigarettes from one of the shelves and gave them to the officer to give to his Toms. The officer thanked me but asked if he could swap them for some Argentine ones – which were also on the shelf. He explained that it could be misunderstood by British Guards if his men were seen to possess British cigarettes.

Fair enough; I gave him a few packs of Lucky Strikes.

Before they departed the shop I ensured that I had my photograph taken with a prisoner. Whenever I show it to anyone I always say, 'That's me with one of my prisoners.'

They're nearly always impressed.

Born at the wrong time
(Goose Green)

While in Goose Green we received mail from home. As company clerk the big blue post sack containing the company's mail was dropped on my doorstep and it was then up to me to sort it out and pass it on to the various platoons that made up our company. Sorting the company mail on the Islands was always a race against the clock. Could I have it sorted before word got around that mail was in? The answer was usually no.

As soon as word was out that the mail was in, I would be swamped by people asking if there was any for them. The first on the scene would normally be the Toms. I would try to explain that their presence and constant questioning was holding me up and that I would be able to get the job done in half the time if they would all just piss off and leave me alone. Next to arrive would be the section CPLs who, being responsible NCOs, would order away the interfering Toms. Once the Toms had gone the CPLs would then start to interfere. Then the platoon sergeants would appear on the scene and, they being senior NCOs, would order the interfering CPLs to go away. Once the CPLs had gone, the sergeants would start to interfere. Finally Jed or Frank would turn up and they would order away the interfering sergeants. Unfortunately there was no one left to order away Jed or Frank, so I would be stuck with them. All of the above mentioned people were of course 'only trying to help', but as soon as they came across a letter with their name on it, they were off into a corner to read.

Once the mail had been sorted and dispatched to its

platoon locations, a few of us sat around the shop reading and rereading our letters. Occasionally information was swapped and any enclosed photos passed between us.

One of our group, a corporal from the Signals Platoon, received a letter from his wife. His wife had given birth to their first child whilst we had been aboard the *Norland* on our journey towards the Falkland Islands. Enclosed with the corporal's letter were photographs of his wife with their first born. He proudly passed the photographs around our group.

Someone, I don't recall who, said it was amazing. He then went over to a large plastic bag which held the personal effects that we had taken from the Argentine dead. The soldier poured the bag's contents on to the floor and began to search amongst the pile of identity cards and letters. He was searching for a letter that he has looked through earlier that day. He found the letter and from it pulled out a set of photographs.

It really was amazing.

The photographs held moments in time when someone, whom we presumed was the dead Argentine's wife, had lain in a hospital bed holding their newborn child. In one of the photographs the dead man's wife, looking tired and bloated but also very happy, was holding in her arms a tiny, wrinkled, squidgy-eyed bundle of new life. The new life was wrapped with a white blanket. The photograph was wrapped with love.

In one hand I held the photograph of the Argentine soldier's wife and her baby. In the other I held the photograph of the British soldier's wife and her baby. I could say that the two photographs were similar but that would be an understatement. They were identical.

When I compared the two images, the newborn life that they contained made me smile. But I was forced to think about how one of the babies was now fatherless, that one of the women was now a widow. I became sad for her and then sad for her baby and then sad for me and then sad for everyone. As we passed the two photographs between us, we all felt a genuine sorrow for the now-widowed Argentine woman and her fatherless child.

For a brief moment we realised what a stupid, wasteful thing we had allowed ourselves to become a part of. Maybe, just for a moment, we even remembered what had always been true: that the Argentine soldiers had wives and they also had babies, just like us.

It made us compassionate.

But our mood of compassion was soon broken. Someone picked up and put on his Hard Man Paratrooper mask. He said that the Argentine woman looked like the sort of girl who would enjoy a good hard fuck up the arse. Someone else said they would like to fuck her in the mouth. Then someone talked about a porno movie they had once seen and we were off.

The next few minutes were filled with various soldiers trying to outdo each other with boasts of what they would like to do to the Argentine woman.

I also boasted.

Today, as I write these words and recall again that period of time in the shop at Goose Green, I try to work out why I once was the way I was. Why I said things about a woman who I had only seconds before been feeling genuinely sorry for. My memory of the two photographs at Goose Green is not a happy one. I am ashamed to think of the words that I spoke. I don't recall exactly what I said about the Argentine woman but I am sure that I said something. Something that I thought to be suitably hard. Something that showed to the others that I was one of them. One of the boys.

If we had been alone, I like to believe that not one of us would have passed comments of a sexual nature about the Argentine woman, but we were not alone, so we behaved in the way that we had been conditioned to behave. Conditioning that was done mostly by ourselves to ourselves.

The wife of a Senior NCO once said to me that, after being around the Army for over fifteen years, she knew of only two types of men within the regiment. She said that there were the ones who were just stupid little boys and the ones who were just nasty little men. She also said that one of the things that the stupid little boys and the nasty little men had in common was that, deep down, they were both cowards.

At the time I did not understand her words, I thought her to be way off the mark. I mean, come on now – how can anyone who goes around stormin' trenches be a coward? He might be a nasty little man and he's most probably exceptionally stupid, but in no way is he a coward.

Today I believe that I now understand her words. Thankfully, when I was in the army, I only got as far as being a stupid little boy. I wasn't around long enough to become a nasty little man.

But I knew a few who were.

Psychiatric day trippers with guns
(Goose Green)

Things were looking up. It was our second day in the shop at Goose Green. I was once again alone, eating my fourth tinned hot dog of the morning and listening to a Simon & Garfunkel cassette on our newly acquired tape machine. The machine in question had been destined to make a one-way trip to Buenos Aires but fortunately along came Frank Pye who, with no thought for his own personal safety, had liberated it from the evil Argentine oppressors and the machine was now alive and well and playing music for the soldiers of democracy. The shop door opened and Jed entered. I could see, just by the expression on his face, that he was a happy man.

'You look happy, sir,' I said. 'Someone died?'

He laughed at my little joke, which only confirmed my previous assessment that he was indeed a happy man. He explained that he had just found a Connie Francis Greatest Hits cassette.

'Connie who?' I asked.

I was soon to find out. Jed walked over to the tape machine, stopped it, took out the tape that was playing and replaced it with Connie. Jed was a warrant officer class 2, I was a private class 1. Bye, bye Paul and Arty. So much for democracy.

My torment began.

As Jed put on the A-side of Connie's greatest for the seventh time that day, things were no longer looking up. I stared blankly out of the window. A group of Argentine prisoners marched past. I thought one of them looked about my size, maybe I could pop him over the head, switch uniforms and spend the rest of the war hiding in the sheep shed with the prisoners. It couldn't be worse than life with Connie.

I made some excuse and departed the shop in search of my new identity. Outside it appeared that the anarchists were still in power. All sorts of noise was coming from the direction of the beach – machine-gun fire, explosions and outbursts of manic laughter. As I crossed a track I narrowly avoided being run over by the Regimental Sergeant-Major who, under the misapprehension that he was Steve McQueen, was charging up and down the settlement on a motorcycle. I thought he was probably looking for a high piece of barbed wire in which to re-enact that scene from *The Great Escape*.

As I continued my own great escape – from Jed, Connie and the shop – I bumped into a friend of mine who was struggling along under the weight of what appeared to be half the captured Argentine weapons at Goose Green; the other half being carried by the soldier behind him. I enquired where he was going with so many guns.

'To the beach, the beach, we're going to the beach,' came his demented reply.

British paratroopers have an almost unhealthy love of weapons, especially weapons they have never fired. I have some more advice for you now and once again it's good advice so try to take it in. Should you ever find yourself with a bored paratrooper on your hands, stick him in a corner, give him a gun, preferably one he's only seen a photo of before, and he'll be as happy as Quentin Crisp on manoeuvres with the marines. Do not under any circumstances give him the ammunition.

So there we were, Goose Green, bit of time on our hands, and lying around just about everywhere are rifles, machine-guns, hand-grenades, packable rocket-launchers, in fact almost the complete Who's Who of death the South American way.

After the events of our first day in the settlement, in which the Falkland Islanders had begun to wish they could return to the peaceful Argentine occupation, the powers that be realised they had a problem on their hands, and passed down the order that if the boys must play with their new toys then would they please go to the beach and do it. The beach was now the official playground: i.e. the official firing range.

Not being averse to letting off a few rounds myself, I helped my friend with his load and off we set in search of the beach. This proved not to be a difficult task; the beach was the place all the noise was coming from.

On reaching our destination, I could not believe it. An Army range is normally a place where you will find the strictest of military discipline. Not on this one. It looked as though the psychiatric wing of a military hospital was holding its annual party on the beach. At least fifty soldiers were on the sands, all of whom were armed to the teeth with automatic weapons, which they were just letting rip with into the sea.

The three of us found a suitable space, put down our loads and began to play. I was in the process of loading another magazine on to the French machine pistol that I had been firing when I noticed the appearance at my side of two soldiers. Between them they were carrying a large wooden crate filled with hand-grenades. They put their crate on the sands, both took a grenade from it, pulled the pins and then threw them into the sea. The grenades exploded and the soldiers broke out into uncontrollable laughter. After about four grenades they obviously got a touch bored so they came up with a new game. It was their own version of cricket: one soldier, who had taken the position of a fielder, took a grenade from the crate, pulled the pin and then threw it to his friend. His friend, the wicket keeper, caught the grenade and then threw it into the sea. The resulting explosion made a much bigger splash than their earlier attempts and, resembling a pair of demented chimps at a tea party, they both jumped up and down laughing and then argued about who was to have the next go. That was enough for me, I was off.

Just as I was leaving, an umpire – in the guise of an officer – arrived on the scene. He gave them both out for insanity before the wicket and told them to pick up their remaining balls and go away. It was without doubt the finest umpiring decision I have ever seen; there was no need for a slow-motion replay.

Someone called my name. I looked over my shoulder and saw a good friend whom I had not seen since the day before the battle. He was part of a group of soldiers huddled in a close circle, carrying out what appeared to be a fiercely argued debate. I walked over to the group, my friend and I shook hands and congratulated each other on our ability to still breathe. The subject under debate was the feasibility of moving one of the Argentine Pack Howitzers down to the beach. No one had ever fired artillery before and this seemed like the perfect opportunity. I was asked if I had ever fired an artillery piece. I thought to myself that even if I had I wouldn't admit it to this debating society. I had the thought that the whole battalion had gone mad. I had the thought that I had also gone mad.

I left the group of unbalanced conspirators to make my way back to the Falklands Branch of the Connie Francis Appreciation Society. Along the way I caught myself singing aloud the words of 'My Happiness'. I stopped, pulled an Argentine Colt .45 pistol from my belt, pressed it against the left side of my brain and jokingly told myself that I was going to die should I ever be caught singing one of Connie's songs again.

I entered the shop just in time to catch the last few bars of 'Stupid Cupid'. More bad news – it was piling on today. Major Jenner and Frank had returned. I had hoped to persuade them to join my 'Connie Out' campaign, but alas, there they were, sitting with Jed, halfway through a bottle of Scotch, singing away and loudly agreeing that they didn't write them like that any more. At least I had found some common ground.

The shop door opened and the padre, Major Cooper, entered. He said in a serious tone of voice that there had been an accident. The tape player was turned off (thank you, Lord) and the padre continued his tale. He explained that an accident had occurred on the beach. Having just returned from the beach I had no problem believing this. He continued to explain that the accident had involved a Royal Marine commando.

'What was he doing this far forward?' interrupted Frank. 'Was he fucking lost?'

'This is not a joking matter, Colour-Sergeant.'

Frank apologised and the padre continued. The marine

in question had been firing an Argentine pistol. After a few rounds he had put the pistol into his belt and leaned over to pick up another weapon. As he leaned over, the pistol had accidently fired and the resulting bullet had removed the top of his penis. I was horrified. Any joke we had ever made at the marines' expense had always been just that, a joke. I felt genuinely sorry for the man. There was more. The marines' commanding officer, on hearing of the man's negligence, a negligence committed in front of Army paratroopers, had ordered that he was to be immediately returned to England and discharged from the service the moment he arrived. I thought this to be somewhat harsh and said so.

'No, it had to be so,' said the padre.

'Why?' I asked.

'Because you have to be a complete prick to be a Royal Marine commando.'

He had taken me hook, line and sinker. Apparently this was an old joke, but I had never heard it before and because it came via our man from the C of E, I never questioned it. Well, that is faith. Isn't it?

Later, near Port Stanley, Jed mysteriously lost his Connie Francis cassette. Someone stole it from his pack and then threw it away.

(Who's sorry now?)

I eat, I shit, I am (3)

One morning, while we occupied the shop at Goose Green, a helicopter arrived carrying an underslung load of fresh bread. The bread had been baked aboard one of the ships of the Task Force and was for the consumption of the local inhabitants of Goose Green. The bread was stacked on a wooden slat, and the wooden slat was placed in the back storeroom of the shop.

The arrival of the bread put me into what is commonly known as a 'No Win' situation. I was given the task of guarding the bread.

That you very fucking much.

I was personally told by the RSM that if anyone from our battalion so much as looked at the bread I was to report them immediately to him. This of course is the sort of command that is fine in theory but not so fine come reality time. For example, when a sergeant walked into the store, noticed the bread and then decided he would have a roll or two, I, as the guard, informed him that the bread was not to be touched. He then informed me that I would need urgent hospital treatment if I didn't shut the fuck up. At this stage I could of course carry out my instructions and report the said sergeant for his crimes against the bread. The RSM would then no doubt bollock the sergeant. The sergeant would then catch up with me, make the rest of my life a misery and also inform all and sundry that I had grassed him up. If, on the other hand, I did not report the sergeant's theft of bread, and the RSM discovered that some of the bread was missing, I was then for the high jump because I had not fulfilled my duty as a guard. As I said, a 'No Win' situation.

Bread was taken, needless to say, but thankfully its disppearance was not noticed.

The introduction of fresh rations into our bodies also had a none-too-pleasant effect on our digestive systems. We got the shits. It happened to all of us at least once. Couldn't be avoided. When it happened to me I was in the shop at Goose Green. If at the end of my life I do get the opportunity to look back, then I shall have no complaints about the situation I found myself in when I got the shits on the Falklands. There was a toilet in the shop, with a seat to rest on. Rolls of toilet paper to wipe my arse with and a chain to pull that made it all go away. As I sat on the toilet in the shop at Goose Green and my arse exploded and the shitty smelly runny green liquid squirted into the pan below I thought about how lucky I was to be sitting there.

Many of us got the shits while on the move, and as they say, 'When you've got to go . . .' You would be walking along when suddenly another soldier would come charging past you. The charging soldier was playing what was known as the 'Shits Game'. The idea was that as soon as you felt movement in your bowels you ran forward as far as you could before your underwear turned to liquid, dropped your pants and let it go. If lucky you would be finished just as your place in the line passed by. Thereby you would not be left behind. The one major drawback with this was that you never really felt like you were finished.

I did in fact get the shits again on the Islands, but thankfully nowhere near as severe as the shits I got in Goose Green and thankfully again not while on the move.

Home, where my love lies . . .
(Goose Green)

It was the early hours of the morning. I was awake, alone and on radio duty in the shop at Goose Green. The night around me was silent and the silence was only occasionally broken by the voices of invisible men as they communicated to each other over the frequencies of war.

On the table before me was a red pen and a writing pad on which I was trying to write a letter to my wife Kathy. I could not write. I was searching for words to describe the events of the past few days but I could not find them. They had been stolen from me, along with a part of my soul, on the battlefield of Goose Green.

I remembered the moment I first saw Kathy as the train she was on slowly drew to a halt before me. I recalled how I'd run along the platform to reach the carriage she was sitting in and again I saw how beautiful she had appeared to me. In my mind I began to play over the first words I had spoken to her and her words to me. I smiled to myself as I thought of our first shared laughter. Once again I tasted the Southern Comfort we had drunk that night, smelled the perfume she'd worn and pictured the clothes she had hidden her beauty behind.

As I sat in the shop I blew a kiss across the ocean and once more experienced the feel of her lips at our first kiss. I became aroused as I remembered the night we had first made love and though 8,000 miles now separated us we made love once more. I began to cry. Tears of joy escaped as I recalled the way she had cried on the night of our wedding and again the next day as we started our journey through life together.

I suddenly felt a deep shame and my tears of joy turned to those of sorrow as I recalled all of the times I had since seen her cry because of me. Because of my actions. My words. I started to laugh aloud at the thought of all the times I had made her laugh and the gentle games of lovers that we had once played strolled across my mind.

I returned to Goose Green and began to whisper her name, feeling that the night winds would carry my words to her in England and that in her dreams she would be able to hear my calls.

I picked up the red pen and began to write. I wrote not of the pains of yesterday but of the joys we would both share on my return. I spoke not of the death that I had seen but of how together we would bring new life into the world.

I mentioned no evil or bad and wrote only of happiness and joy. My love for her floated from my body on to the paper. I wrote a love letter. The only true love letter I have ever written.

Later, that same night, as I lay awake in my sleeping-bag I began to feel loneliness. I did not wish to sleep alone that night. I wanted to sleep with Kathy. I wanted to be in a safe, dark place with her and have her wipe the sorrow from my mind. I wanted to go home. I wanted to be where Kathy was.

Cigarette smokers in black plastic bags
(Goose Green)

At Goose Green my battalion had killed over 250 Argentines. Before me now were maybe 30 or 40 of their corpses. They were laid in a row, the same way that exhibits are laid out in a gallery and, as with a gallery, there were people passing among them, taking photographs and discussing the exhibits. I too joined the procession.

A tractor arrived, pulling behind it another trailerload of dead. The new exhibits were unloaded from the trailer and they were added to the growing line of corpses. As I stood before the casualties of war I was trying to tell myself that before me there was a pile of dead people. I felt as though some great mystery of life should now reveal itself to me. I should now understand something that I had been unable to understand before. There was no revelation. There was no understanding. I felt nothing.

One of the dead had once been a Pucara pilot who had been shot down during the battle. He was now just a pile of red flesh. He had no head. He had no arms. He had no nothing except for a leg. He still had a leg – with a boot on.

I have a friend who has a photograph of the dead Pucara pilot at Goose Green. Should these words ever be published, I would not like the photograph to be printed alongside. I could find no words to write underneath it.

I saw many soldiers lying next to the corpses while their friends took happy snaps of them. One soldier picked up a dead Argentine, supported the corpse's weight underneath his arm, put a cigarette in the dead man's mouth, then one in his own. He then held a lighter under the corpse's cigarette and his friend took a photograph. They both laughed. I also laughed.

This was foolish – smoking can kill.

Two soldiers, who were not paratroopers, were one by one putting the dead men into body bags. With one corpse they were having difficulty. The dead man's elbow was pointed skywards and his hand still gripped the clothing around his wound. Because of the protruding elbow, they could not fit the corpse into its bag. An officer from my battalion approached. He noticed the struggling soldiers and told them to move aside. He got to his knees, drew a knife from his belt and cut the material around the dead man's gripping hand. He then tried to straighten the corpse's elbow. It would not straighten. The officer got to his feet and began to kick the elbow down. After a few kicks the arm straightened and the men put him into his allotted bag. We all had a job to do that day. Theirs was to put dead men into black plastic bags.

A few days later I stood in a line of men, waiting for a helicopter that was to fly us to Fitzroy. On the ground, lying in a puddle of mud, was a human foot. The foot was naked and had been blown off just above the ankle. It had once been attached to the body of an Argentine soldier who had been killed by an explosion that occurred while he and his comrades were moving ammunition away from their prison shed. One of the soldiers had nearly burned to death in the accident. He did not burn to death because he was shot first. When the ammunition exploded he was caught in a fire-ball. No one could reach him.

His screams were heard over the whole settlement and a medic who had tried to pull him from the flames shot him four times to relieve him of his pain.

The medic could not sit by him. He could not hold his

hand, he had no time to ask his Lord for understanding and he was unable to shoot him through the brain. I know this though: the medic was a hero, he was the bravest man I had ever seen.

As I looked as the naked foot, a soldier broke ranks from our line and disappeared behind a hedgerow. During his absence one of his friends ran over to the foot and picked it up. Another soldier opened the missing man's bergen and took out his sleeping-bag. The bag was unzipped and unrolled and the foot was placed inside. The sleeping-bag was wrapped up and placed back into the bergen. We all laughed. It was a very funny thing to see.

I laugh no more at this – it no longer seems very funny.

Some of the photographs of the dead men at Goose Green made their way onto the walls of the corporal's mess in Aldershot. One night I was at the bar with my wife. Kathy went over to look at the photographs hanging on the walls. She immediately returned to the bar and said she would like to go. I asked why, because I had just bought two drinks. She explained that the photographs were sick and she had no wish to remain in a room that had such sick things on its walls. Kathy was right; the photographs were sick.

War is also sick.

Many of you who have just read the above words may be judging the soldiers who played games with and took photographs of the corpses of war. Please try not to. If young men are sent 8,000 miles from their homes, to fight a war in a place that none of them had ever heard of, then such things should be expected. Their bravado was just a cover for their fear. Their actions were brought about by the conditioning they had received, at the expense of someone's taxes, to be able to fight, fight hard, and be sure that they would win.

Win for you also.

The Bible says: 'He that is without sin among you, let him first cast a stone.'

Here endeth the lesson.

We interrupt this war to bring you a message from our sponsors.

'Hi, Combat Ken here. Let me tell you, war is tough. I know, I was at Goose Green, I saw my friends die, I could have died myself. That's why it was always reassuring to know that as a soldier in the British Army, only the best, the very best, was good enough for me. British Army Body Bags – I wouldn't be found dead in anything else.'

Is that a take?

Really flying, nearly dying, Toms on stag (Fitzroy)

Sixty-two of us boarded a Chinook helicopter at Goose Green. We were going to Fitzroy. Chinooks are not meant to carry so many men – trouble was, we all knew it. We stood in the helicopter, all with full kit, all carrying four 81mm mortar rounds.

As the helicopter lifted into the air and began its forward movement I tried not to think of the obviously suicidal Argentine Air Force that had shown its courage to us all over the waters of San Carlos.

A colour-sergeant standing next to me called out,

'Fuckin' typical. The only time I want a fuckin' parachute and the bastards won't give me one.'

Once again we all laughed.

After what seemed like another lifetime we finally reached Fitzroy. Two patrols from our recce platoon had flown into the settlement earlier that day to confirm the absence of 'baddies' and to secure a landing zone.

I read in a book that the Chinook that flew me to Fitzroy was very nearly shot down. Very nearly shot down by British forces. As the Chinook flew low-level over the Falklands landscape it was spotted by one of our forward observation posts. The men of the observation post radioed the men at Task Force HQ whose job it was to know everything about everything and asked, 'Do we have a Chinook flying over Fitzroy?'

'No,' replied the men who knew everything about everything, 'the only Chinook we have is at Goose Green, ferrying prisoners.'

So the men at the observation post radioed the men of the Royal Artillery and gave them the grid reference and a fire order for our landing zone in Fitzroy.

Meanwhile, I'm on the Chinook helicopter and I'm worrying about the Argentine Air Force?

Thankfully another group of men saw our helicopter land and noticed that it carried British markings. They had heard the fire order being given over the net and so in turn got on the radio and called a halt to it.

Thank you very much.

The Chinook, before we boarded it, had been at Goose Green ferrying prisoners out to a waiting ship at sea. But a Brigadier, who was proud to tell of his bold decision at a filmed news conference, took command of the Chinook, or to use his exact words, 'We grabbed it, and shoved as many soldiers as we could into that Chinook.' He then ordered it to be dispatched to Fitzroy. It would have been a very good plan if only someone had thought to tell the men whose job it was to know everything about everything, back at Task Force HQ.

Once in Fitzroy we made ourselves comfortable by moving into the settlement's community centre. Once settled, I paired up with Ray and the two of us set off to have a look around. Major Jenner, Jed, Frank and the rest of company HQ had stayed at Goose Green but had kindly volunteered my services for the move forward. Come to think of it – I can't believe I still talk to these people!

As Ray and I walked through Fitzroy we came across a small group of Falkland Islanders. One of them, a man who I would have guessed was in his late thirties, wore a cowboy hat. This wouldn't have been too bad if it had been a proper cowboy hat, but it wasn't, it was a cardboard one. I had once owned a very similar hat. It had been bought for me from the toy department at Woolworth's, by my mother, when I was going through my Cowboys and Indians phase. To go with the hat the Falkland Islander also wore a star-shaped silver plastic badge on the right lapel of his jacket. Written on the badge, in big bold letters, was the word 'Sheriff'.

'I'm the Sheriff,' said the Falkland Islander.

'I'm very happy for you,' said I.

The Sheriff then pulled a toy cowboy pistol from the belt around his waist. He held out the toy pistol, warned us that it was loaded, with caps, and asked if we would like to have a go with it. We declined his offer and also declined his request to let him have a go with our guns.

One of the other Islanders, completely out of the blue, blurted out the statement, 'I've got six sheep.'

'Really?' said Ray. 'Why didn't you tell us you were a pimp?'

We both laughed. The Islander asked what a pimp was.

As we walked away from the Islanders I caught myself thinking about the Galapagos Islands.

After a quick lap around the settlement Ray and I both returned to the community centre. One of the Islanders produced a 16mm film projector and some films to go with it.

'Got any porn?' he was asked almost in unison.

The projector was set up and a film was shown. The film in question was *Von Ryan's Express*, starring Frank Sinatra. It's a war movie – well what else? This to me was a great coincidence; *Von Ryan's Express* had been the last movie I had watched in the NAAFI at Browning Barracks, before completing my basic training.

I mentioned this to those around me. Someone said that he wouldn't want to be me: 'That's a bad omen that is, Luke. If I were you I'd be worried that it also turns out to be the last film you ever see.'

I really could live without comments like that.

Later that night Ray and I were sent out to one of the 'stag' positions. After a bit of searching we eventually found the place that we had to guard and relieved the two soldiers who were on duty. They handed over to us a radio, an IWS night sight and then said their farewells.

The night was cold and the thought of having to spend two hours out in it was not a pleasant one. On the other hand we had seen it all before and had stagged on for longer periods of time in colder, and harder circumstances, both in training and while in Northern Ireland. Always being the alert one – or the one who worried the most, they amount to the same thing – I was constantly having images of Argentine Special Forces creeping up on us. We knew from Goose Green that their night sight equipment was far superior to ours and that to any would-be Argentine attacker we would have been sitting targets. So we put about twenty yards between us and buried ourselves into a hedgerow.

After about an hour the cold of night began to take effect and each passing minute stretched to what seemed like ten. I went over to where Ray lay and said I could do with a hot drink. We both wore webbing and so carried everything that was needed to get a brew on. The drawback was the light the flames from our cookers would make. After a short discussion and a little 'Airborne Initiative' we schemed a solution. We picked up the radio and night sight and walked a few yards back into the settlement. We found a garage. The garage was locked with a padlock Using a bayonet we broke the padlock and entered. It was perfect. No windows and it was empty. Ray returned to the stag position while I stayed in the garage and boiled some water. Once boiled I made two mugs of tea and carried them out to Ray.

As we sat in Fitzroy, surrounded by the darkness, shivering with cold, the tea I was holding warmed me. It cheered me up. Not only for the warmth it gave, but also for the way it made me feel: I had won a little victory. Got away with something.

When our time on stag was over and two other soldiers arrived to replace us, I took one of them to the garage, and showed him the score. It was now a place for the use of Toms on stag.

Later, during the same period of darkness, and our second period of stag Ray and I went to guard three Argentine prisoners who were being held in one of the settlement's sheep sheds. The Argentines, two officers and one private soldier, were members of the Argentine Air Force.

Before arriving in Fitzroy they had been working as forward spotters on one of the hills around Goose Green. After we had captured Goose Green they had been cut off from their unit. In an attempt to reach Port Stanley they had laid up for a few days, then somehow got their hands on a civilian Land-Rover and using the Land-

Rover had attempted to drive cross-country to Port Stanley and safety.

Someone, somewhere along the route spotted them and we were forewarned of their expected arrival in Fitzroy. A patrol was sent out in ambush. A few hours later the patrol returned with the three Argentine prisoners and their Land-Rover in tow.

The three of them were interrogated by our intelligence section and then put in a pen, within one of the sheep sheds. When Ray and I went to guard them, I would guess that we were the third or fourth pair of guards they had had that night.

We soon found out that the two officers both spoke English, one of them fluently. The pen that held them had a gate, but the gate had no lock. The pen could have been broken out of very easily and was really only being used to mark territory: where they could go and where they could not. We began to talk to the two officers through the wooden bars of the pen. They told us who they were and what their job had been at Goose Green. I had the thought that before me now were the men who were responsible for the accuracy of the shell-fire that had rained down on us all day at Goose Green.

While we talked to the two officers, the private soldier lay resting on a pile of sheep's wool to the rear of their pen. Within our first few minutes of conversation we offered, and then made, some hot coffee for the prisoners.

When we passed the coffee to one of the officers he thanked us, and then walked over to where the private soldier lay and offered him the drink. We took note of this. We liked the Argentine officer for it. He looked after his Toms.

For the next two hours we stood standing, four men together, talking through a wooden cage. Two with guns and two without.

One of them said that he had been impressed by our

helicopter pilots. While holed up in the hills he had watched a British helicopter land nearby. He said he was amazed; the weather conditions and visibility were so bad he couldn't believe that our pilots would fly. He went on to say that Argentine helicopter pilots would be more suited to flying at fun fairs. This made me laugh.

They asked if we knew what would be done with them. We said that all we knew was that according to 'Rumour Control' the Argentine prisoners we had captured at Goose Green were being ferried out to ships and that the ships were going to take them to Ascension Island. We told them that we thought this was also what would happen to them.

They asked us if we had been to Ascension Island and if we knew of its climate. We told them that we had and it was hot. We laughed together when someone said that they were better off going there than we were to where we were going.

While we talked to the two Argentines, distant sounds of constant shelling played in the background. Faraway thuds and bangs. The shell-fire was coming from our ships at sea and was being directed at Port Stanley. I think this was mainly being done to ensure that no one in Port Stanley ever got a good night's sleep.

At one point in the conversation Ray and I were fishing for compliments from the two Argentine officers. They had watched the battle of Goose Green from a hill and so we wanted to hear from them just exactly how bloody wonderful everyone and everything to do with the British Parachute Regiment was. The Argentines agreed with us that we were indeed fine soldiers, but, despite this fact, we would never capture Port Stanley. They said it was too well defended, by too many men who had had weeks to prepare for our attack. We were having none of this and told them so. It was just as Ray was telling them that we of the Parachute Regiment were the bravest, toughest soldiers the world had ever seen, that a shell whistled in outside and a loud explosion ripped through the night. Ray and I both automatically hit the deck and crawled towards where our helmets lay.

To us it was Argentine counter-attack time.

Then once again – nothing happened. Still lying on the floor, helmets on, weapons cocked, we turned to look at the three Argentines. The two officers were still standing on the same spot. The private still slept where he had been sleeping. As the two Argentines were officers, we turned to them for an explanation of the explosion.

'Well obviously,' replied one of them, 'your ships are shelling Porto Argentina, one of the shells fired was faulty in some way, it strolled from its projectory and landed outside this shed.'

He then said that we should try to calm down a bit. Try and relax. Not worry so much.

I turned to Ray and asked if he would like to shoot them or should I.

Then all four of us laughed.

When our time on stag was over and our two replacements arrived, we shook hands with the two Argentine officers and the four of us wished each other well for the future.

Since that night in Fitzroy I have often thought of the two Argentine officers whom we spent two hours guarding. I regret that today I cannot recall their names or any other details about them, but it has always been a dream of mine that one day I shall meet them again. Part of my dream is that they are no longer officers in the Argentine Air Force and that I no longer carry a gun. I also dream that our conversation is not carried out through bars.

A wise man once wrote, 'If you don't have a dream, if you don't have a dream, then how you gonna have a dream come true.'

So I shall continue to dream.

Gullible, gallant, laughing heroes
(Fitzroy)

Loads of trouble. The whole forward movement of the Falklands Task Force is in jeopardy. The Toms of 2 Para have got a dog on. To be fair – and I do try to be fair – I shall give both sides of the story.

Our side, in para-speak:

We were at Goose Green, right. Shit's flying all day, we're in trouble. Trouble like you wouldn't believe. One of the companies is bogged down up against fuck knows what, they're up shit creek without a condom, i.e. loads of bodies, no forward movement. Jones has gone fuckin' mental, stormed to the front, turned it all around, gotten himself blown away and Keeble, the second-in-command, he takes over. Come the night, we've pushed 'em back into their little Porto Fucking Goose Green or whatever the fuck they called it, we can see the place and we've got the fuckers boxed in. Next day brother Argie suddenly decides he'd much rather be our friend, everything's sweet and as far as the Toms are concerned Keeble's now the new boss man.

Few days later we're all told that Whitehall or some other bunch of shitheads – who gives a toss – have decided that we need a new colonel and Keeble's going back to being second-in-command.

Their side of the story: we couldn't give a fuck. (Told you I was fair.)

We had reached Fitzroy. Word was passed down that the new colonel had arrived. During the previous night he had flown from the base on Ascension Island and parachuted into the night sea. The order was given for us to gather in the community centre; the new colonel wished to speak to the heroes of his new command. As we sat on the wooden floor of the hall the whispered conversations began.

'Who the fuck's this Cadbury's Milk Tray Man then?'

'Dunno, never fuckin' heard of him.'

'Can't see why they need to send the cunt out, Keeble's done all right, don't seem right that we should have to put up with this new wanker.'

'Yeah, too fuckin' true.'

The RSM entered the room and called for the hall to sit up. We all sat up. The new colonel walked in. Under one of his arms he carried a pile of newspapers.

'They've sent us a fucking newspaper boy.'

We hated him. Never met him, never seen him, never even heard of him, but we hated him.

The new colonel began to speak. He told us how he had just come from England, and how everyone back home now knew the name of 2 Para. Our heroic exploits at Goose Green had set the nation on fire, we were the united toast of Britain. From his jacket he pulled a sack of telegrams and messages that the battalion had received. Most of them were addressed to 'The Gallant Men of the Second Paras'. Everyone had sent praise for our deeds and condolences for our dead. The colonel read words from the Queen, praise from Prince Charles and, 'That's my boys', from Margaret Thatcher. The boys loved that one: we were famous.

'Hey, I'm a fucking hero.'

'If that lot's not worth a few shags when I get home, then I don't know what the fuck is.'

One by one the colonel held up editions of the British newspapers for the day after Goose Green. He read aloud the headlines from each one. They all referred to us as heroes. We were heroes. Everyone at home was proud of us, they all wanted to buy us a drink. By the time the colonel got to his pièce de résistance, i.e. the *Sun*, pages

1-18, centre photo-spread, Page Three girl wearing a Parachute Regiment beret, all under the headline, 'Hero Paras Massacre Dirty Argie Bastards', the mood among the men in the hall was rapidly changing.

'This new colonel's not such a bad old cunt after all, is he?'

'No, obviously seems to know what he's talking about.'

As the colonel read aloud from the *Sun*, people just couldn't restrain their joy any longer. Everyone began smiling to each other in a 'who's a good boy then' sort of way. Laughter broke out in the ranks with the officers once more leading the charge. By the time the colonel got to the Page Three girl that had always wanted a paratrooper boyfriend, soldiers were clapping and cheering aloud at the end of each sentence.

'Hey, Beast, you wanna send the dog a photo of you with your cock hanging out, even an ugly bastard like you might get a fuck.'

Everyone heard, everyone laughed.

The colonel finally finished his reading, told us all once again what an honour it was for him to be given the job of leading men such as us, and off he went.

'What a fine man that new colonel is.'

'Yeah, no doubt about it.'

'Did you hear he jumped in – he's a right fucking mental warrie bastard, he is.' (Highest possible compliment in para-speak.)

'Give you six to four he don't make Stanley.'

'If he's as mad as the last one he won't make fucking breakfast.'

The man who had entered the room being hated had left being loved. His name was Chaundler.

He's a brigadier now.

He was the one that took over after Jonesie got blown away.

Nasty, negligent, unbalanced minds
(Fitzroy)

I rolled up my sleeping-bag, packed it into my bergen and made my way outside.

I couldn't believe outside – the war had caught up.

As I walked from the shed I was overcome with what I can only describe as a feeling of 'cinematography': I felt as though I had just stepped into a movie. There were no longer only sixty-two of us in the settlement of Fitzroy. A Sea King helicopter carrying an underslung load flew over my head from behind the shed; the surrounding high ground was covered with moving soldier ants, all of whom were digging holes. On one of the tracks through Fitzroy were two Scorpion light tanks. I didn't even know we had such things on the islands. I knew the Argentines did. We had been told of them, seen photographs of them and watched them on film aboard the *Norland*. The two Scorpions were a very reassuring sight. There were also soldiers all over the settlement and more arriving via the quay in the bay to my right. Docked at the far end of the bay were two large ships. I wondered which ships they were. I would later find out. The whole world was to later find out.

A few hours on, that same morning, I found myself aboard a trailer that was being pulled by a tractor. The supplies from the two ships in the bay were being unloaded on to a nearby beach. The banks surrounding the beach were too steep for vehicles to climb and so bodies were required to help dig an easier path up through the bank. The tractor followed a track from Fitzroy that ran above but also along the water's edge.

113

At one point we met a steep bank. I just presumed that the tractor would stop, we would get out and the tractor would attempt to climb the bank without us as a burden. I was wrong. The tractor did not stop, it continued to move forward and with the greatest of ease climbed straight up the bank. We all slid to the rear of the trailer. I was truly amazed. Impressed even. I had never realised how powerful tractors were.

After we had completed the digging I returned to the settlement and made my way along the jetty that stretched out into the bay. Sat on the wooden floor, with his legs dangling over the side, was a good friend of mine. I had not seen him since we had all been dug in on Sussex Mountain. As I recognised him I called his name, and jokingly shouted: 'Not fucking dead yet!'

I sensed it before I saw his face – he was sad, very sad. I asked what was troubling him.

He took his gaze from the water, looked at me, and said: 'I've shot someone, Luke.'

I sat down next to my friend and in my best 'I understand' voice, began to spell out the old 'Him or You' number.

'You don't understand,' he said. 'The soldier I shot, he wasn't Argentine, he was a Royal Engineer. I had a negligent discharge.'

On hearing this, I felt for my friend. I knew that all of us, if we were honest, would admit that we lived in fear of having a negligent discharge, especially with an SMG, which was the weapon my friend carried. If cocked, an SMG only needs to be dropped to set it off.

Unfortunately not all of us are able to be honest.

A sergeant approached. He noticed my friend, stopped, crouched down and pushed his face into the face of my friend. The sergeant's verbal negligent discharge began. Anybody would have expected a little dig in jest, but the sergeant was not jesting. He was nasty, just plain, ignorant, human-being nasty. As my friend's face went from shame to anger, I gripped his arm and whispered, 'Just ignore the fucker.'

Eventually the sergeant stopped his verbal diarrhoea and made his way back along the jetty. I could not stop myself from feeling anger for my friend. I stared at the sergeant's back and was overcome with hatred, real hatred. I had never experienced that emotion before and have only once since. I wanted to shoot him. I wanted to kill him.

Today, as I write these words, I no longer wish to shoot and kill the sergeant. I believe his mind to have been unbalanced, that's all. He was just a sick man with an unbalanced mind.

I was also just a sick man with an unbalanced mind. We were all just sick men with unbalanced minds. The real pity was – we all had guns.

Almost a year after the encounter on the jetty in Fitzroy, I was working as a clerk in the battalion orderly room in Aldershot. I was behind with my work and so had gone into the offices on a Saturday afternoon in an attempt to catch up. On one of the desks in the offices was a metal box. In the metal box were the battalion's Senior NCO's Regimental Conduct Sheets. A Regimental Conduct Sheet is a piece of paper which holds details of all disciplinary charges brought against a soldier during his military career. The metal box contained the ones for sergeants and above. Loads of secrets.

I love a good read.

Without needing to even think I let my fingers do the walking and pulled out SGT Nasty's Conduct Sheet. I read his charges. One of them was due spent, which basically meant the penance had been served, all was forgiven and the charge was crossed out in red ink. I held the sheet of paper up to the light and read the forgotten charge. Then, quoting the words of another sick person, with an exceptionally unbalanced mind, I called aloud, 'Gotcha!'

During the 1970s, in a guardroom in Northern Ireland, Sergeant Nasty had had a negligent discharge with a Browning 9mm pistol. So then I said to myself, 'If Downing Street can leak, then why can't the Battalion Orderly room of 2 Para?' I should have been a civil servant – I chose my pigeons well.

That Monday, ten o'clock in the NAAFI, I pulled up a chair and sat down with three others. I leaned forward and whispered, 'Hey, listen, don't tell a soul, but you know SGT Nasty . . .'

A few days later in the same NAAFI a soldier came over to the table I was sitting at. He pulled up a chair, sat down, and, to my immense satisfaction, told me all about SGT Nasty's negligent discharge in Northern Ireland. Even though I was satisfied to hear the news was spreading I did have the thought that I might now be LCPL Nasty.

Who's a sick man with an unbalanced mind then? Most boys. That's who.

Welsh pornographic Mars bars
(Bluff Cove/Fitzroy)

I was in a very large sheep shed at Fitzroy. The whole battalion was in a very large sheep shed at Fitzroy. I was wondering whose madness had been responsible for putting so many men into one building while a full-scale war was happily raging away outside.

It seemed everyone that I spoke to that day, officers and men alike, were also sharing my thoughts, but still we remained in the shed.

The air suddenly filled with the sound of approaching jets. Machine-gun fire began to ring out; there were two loud explosions and I instantly felt fear. I ran to the nearest exit and was soon standing at the water's edge behind the shed.

Docked in the bay before me were two ships; flames and smoke poured skywards from their decks. All of us began to run along the shore to the point nearest the burning ships.

The scene before us was one of chaos and horror. Helicopters were flying into the smoke above the burning ships in an attempt to winch people from the decks. There were men jumping from the decks into the water and many others who were already trying to swim to the shore. Life-rafts of every type were also in the water and one helicopter pilot was trying to use the wind from his rotor blades to push a rubber lifecraft away from the heat of the burning ships. Lying on the beach were men suffering from burns and shock. Medics were running between them frantically trying to assist. I ran into the water and joined a row of men pulling on a rope that was attached to a lifeboat. In the boat there were men whose expressions and cries I can still see and hear today.

We began to lift the men from the craft and place them on the sand alongside their comrades. After a time some form of order was restored and we began to make our way back to the sheep shed. On my return journey I met a corporal from C Company. We stopped and exchanged a few words and from his equipment he pulled out a magazine. It was a Danish pornographic magazine.

He asked if I would like to borrow it. I said thank you, promised not to stick the pages together and we parted company. A few yards further on nature called so I stopped where I was, dropped my trousers, squatted down and began to flick through the magazine. From time to time I looked up from the naked bodies and took in the carnage that was still unfolding around me.

I looked back to the magazine, turned a page and there in full glorious technicolour was the most obscene photograph I had ever seen. I stretched out my arms and began to turn the magazine in an attempt to work out who was where and what bits of flesh belonged to whom. I thought to myself, 'This is obscene.' I again looked away from the magazine and saw two badly burnt Welsh soldiers in tears being helped along a track to the First Aid Post. I thought that was also obscene.

I can recall thinking, as my eyes passed between the two obscenities, how all those fine upstanding people back home would be organising committees and holding protest meetings should the magazine I was holding ever become available at their local newsagents. Yet, on the same day, they seemed only too happy to send their sons off to fight a war, 8,000 miles from their newsagents, in a place that none of them had ever heard of.

This was of course being far too harsh on the fine upstanding people back home, but maybe you can understand what my mind was trying to say. I turned back to the magazine and began to read the literary masterpiece, 'Hans off Gretel'. Something winged passed my ear. I dived to the ground and with my trousers around my ankles crawled into cover. After a short space of time I stuck my head above ground level to try and see where the 'something' had come from. The ships in the bay were burning with a vengeance and the ammunition they were carrying had joined the party. I decided to go back to the sheep shed.

I pulled up my trousers and began to play Olympic athlete. By the time I reached the shed it was overflowing with vacant-looking Welsh soldiers and the odd, badly shaken, Chinese. They looked as though they had all lost their souls. They sat in complete silence.

The silence of the shed that day was the loudest noise I have ever heard. I brewed a mug of tea and began to share it with the soldiers around me. By this time their combined sadness was beginning to rub off on me, so in an attempt to lift my spirits, I thought let's have some chocolate. If life's a piece of shit when you look at it, eat some chocolate, it can help. I found my bergen and reached into one of its side pouches in search of my Mars bars. They were gone. This was not good news and I became angry, very angry. I automatically turned to the people around me in search of the culprit.

In one of the corners of the shed, sitting on the floor and wrapped in a blanket, was a Welsh soldier. From the blanket protruded a hand and in the hand was a Mars bar. As far as I was concerned, my Mars bar. This one was going to wish he was back on the *Galahad* by the time I was finished; I was going to introduce him to a level of violence he had only seen in comic books.

I made my move towards him. As I did, he started to cry aloud. The Mars bar fell from his grip and his head sank into his knees. I stopped, felt the sorrow that surrounded him and decided that I could probably make it through the day minus a work, rest and play bar.

I returned to where my equipment lay and put a cassette into the player that Frank had brought from Goose Green. I pressed the play button and turned up the volume. A short space of time went by when suddenly my company major turned on me with a ferocity that shocked me.

He told me to turn the music off immediately, which I did, and he walked away. I turned to the nearest soldier and, while pointing my head in the general direction of the major, asked: 'What the fuck's his problem?'

The soldier advised me to listen to the song that I had just put on. I picked up the machine, placed one of its speakers to my ear, turned the volume to low and pressed the play button. I wanted to hear the offending song and find out why the major had gone seemingly insane. The cassette was *Queen's Greatest Hits*.

These are the words to the song that I played aloud that day. Aloud, around the sheep shed in Fitzroy. The sheep shed that was filled with men who had just seen their friends burn to death. Men who had been lucky to escape the same fate themselves:

'Boom, boom, boom, boom, another one bites the dust!'

It was I who had been insane, not the major.

Exceptionally truthful bad taste
(Fitzroy)

Shortly after the *Galahad* had been hit I sat on the floor of the sheep shed. I was happily constructing my latest bit of torture for the recruiting office sergeant in Bristol, while cleaning my weapon for the second time that day. I started to sing aloud a song. I finished the song, went right back to its beginning and began to sing it again, but this time I changed a few words as I went along. Ten minutes later my musical masterpiece was complete and I set off in search of an audience. I found it in the form of Support Company Headquarters and the Battalion's Assault Engineer Platoon.

It was a big hit. I left to rapturous applause and laughter.

The song in question was the Beatles' 'Yesterday'.

Please listen: I will sing my Falklands version of it for you:

Yesterday, all my troubles seemed so far away,
Then they came and blew the Welsh away,
Oh I believe in yesterday.

Suddenly, he's not half the man he used to be,
He lost his left leg just below the knee,
The Argie Jets came suddenly.

Why the fuck I'm here, I don't know, must be insane.
Is there something wrong?
Yes, napalm is heading my way.

Yesterday, life was such an easy game to play,
Now I need a place to hide away,
Oh how I wish it was yesterday.

Sick or what?
A few years after my re-composing of the Lennon and McCartney song in Fitzroy I sang it to a girlfriend. She said it was in exceptionally bad taste. I said that she was probably right, but she should try to remember that it was also exceptionally truthful.

I really had wished it was yesterday.

Wouldn't you?

Praying, claustrophobic, plane spotters
(Fitzroy/Bluff Cove)

I was still in a very large sheep shed at Fitzroy, though
the whole battalion was no longer with me. The air
attack on the two ships in the bay had convinced the
powers that be that maybe it was not such a good idea to
have a whole battalion in one building while a war raged
outside. The order was soon passed down that we were to
move to the hills and dig in. Except for me. Yank, me
and a handful of others were to remain in the shed and
protect the battalion's equipment from the newly-arrived
hordes of Welsh bandits.

As Yank and I sat on the shed floor, sharing a mug of
tea, he commented on how different war was to an
exercise; that had we been in England we would have
been only too happy to wave goodbye to our comrades as
they set off for the rain and wind of the hills while we
remained in the relative comfort of a shed. We cursed
our luck for being ordered to remain behind.

I heard them first. I grabbed Yank by the arm and
said: 'Jets.'

'It'll only be the fucking RAF, arriving three hours
after the event again,' he replied.

The air once more filled with the crackling of machine-
gun fire. Something large, nasty and noisy flew over the
top of the shed. I was once again gripped by panic and
charged towards the nearest door in an attempt to get
out of the building. As I reached the shed door I pulled
myself to a grinding halt. My escape route had a hundred
red tracer bullets cutting across it. I automatically
turned on my heels and ran back across the shed in

search of another exit. Bullets began to rip through the side of the tin shed, I dived to the floor and crawled up against another soldier who was lying under a large wooden trolley.

I cannot recall which one of us starting saying aloud the Lord's Prayer, but I do remember that by the second line we were both praying. A never-ending stream of bullets flew over our heads, I put my hands over my ears to try and cut out the deafening noise that the bullets were making as they ripped through the walls and ricocheted around the shed. The amount of fire was so heavy that the thought flashed through my mind that outside there must be a Pucara flying over, with a drum machine-gun, putting down a bullet every six inches of its path.

I do not know for how long the two of us lay on that sheep shed floor. The only measure of time that I have is that up to that point I had been alive for twenty-three years and it was longer than that.

The shooting finally stopped and we hesitantly crawled out from under the trolley and made our way outside. We stopped the first passing soldier and asked what had happened. He explained that the Argentine jets had returned to have another go at the ships and unlike their first visit of the day the welcoming committee had been a touch more organised. As the jets passed across the horizon the soldiers on the hills surrounding the bay had opened fire.

The jets' path along the horizon had taken them behind the shed that we had been in and, as they passed, the legally-armed psychopaths on the hills had followed with their weapons. The nasty noisy thing that had flown over the roof of the shed had been a Blowpipe missile, a Blowpipe missile fired by our own troops. The bullets that had ripped through the shed and pinned us praying to the floor had been British bullets, it had been friendly fire.

I know something else: friendly fire isn't very.

Today, as I write these words, I am able to understand that the events of that day have left me with one of my deepest mental scars. If I now ever find myself in a building and I hear the sound of an approaching jet, I feel, be it only for a few seconds, a sudden rush of panic. I remember exactly how I felt that day; I experience once again the thoughts I held as I lay under that trolley. I always catch myself beginning to run out of the building.

I know another song. It goes like this: 'I'm leaving on a jet plane, don't know when I'll be back again.'

Good.

Boys with views on the men with news
(Fitzroy)

The Toms were well pissed off.

'Fucking Jewish bastards. Who the fuck do they think they are?'

'Yeah, and the fucking BBC. Bunch of cunts. Shitheads gave the game away at Goose Green and now this fucking shit.'

We were in Fitzroy. It was dark. We had moved back down off the hills and into the sheep shed for the night. We believed the Argentine Air Force to be like Indians – they didn't attack at night. I was part of a group of men standing outside the shed. We were waiting. With us stood Robert Fox, the BBC man. He held a small transistor radio, tuned into the BBC World Service. We were awaiting the news on the hour. We were hoping to hear something new. About us.

The radio emitted six pips. It was the only noise in the darkness of Fitzroy. After the sixth pip, a voice announced that we were listening to the World News from the BBC. It was time to hear about us.

The voice on the radio continued. 'Israeli forces have invaded the Lebanon.'

'What?' We went mental. It felt like a great betrayal. How could the BBC put what the Israelis were doing in the Lebanon before what we were doing in the Falklands?

The BBC were pushing their luck with us. At Goose Green they had given the game away by announcing on the news that a paratrooper battalion had broken out of the beach-head and was heading towards Goose Green, and now this.

When the BBC announced to the world that we were about to attack Goose Green we were holed up in battalion strength around a house at Camilla Creek. We had arrived during darkness. A few of us found some shelter in a small generator shed. It was cramped and uncomfortable but it was in the dry and out of the wind. Because it was a generator shed, within it there was an engine, and because there was an engine, on the floor there was lots of oil. I got oil marks on my beret that night – at the time it pissed me off severely, but by the same time next day I didn't give a shit.

As soon as the news of our impending attack was announced over the radio we had to leave the generator shed and move away from the ground around the house at Camilla Creek. We moved off into a gully. Into the wind. Into the rain. It was not appreciated. As Robert Fox was 'Our man from the BBC' he was asked to explain why the BBC had betrayed us. He said that the announcement on the news was as big a surprise to him as it was to us and he asked us to believe that he had had nothing to do with it.

Colonel Jones said he'd sue.

In Fitzroy, on hearing the BBC relegating us to second place on the world news, behind the Israelis, we all once again turned on Robert Fox. He explained that the BBC World Service News was just that – World News and that to the majority of people on the planet what we the British were up to was not the be-all and end-all of their existence.

We could just about see the logic to that.

In Port Stanley a few days after the war was over I was aboard a ship that was docked in the harbour. I was part of a line of men who were queueing to use a satellite phone to call home on. As I waited, a journalist, who was not known to any of us, walked past our queue and stood at the front. He turned and explained that he had an important dispatch to send to his paper and that he hoped we didn't mind but he was going to have to push in.

We replied that we hoped he didn't mind, but if he did that, we were going to have to push his face in for him. He was then told to fuck off to the back of the queue. Not knowing when he was beat the journalist then tried to pull rank on us. (The hero members of the British press attached to the Task Force had all been given honorary officer rank. We had also all been instructed to treat them as such, even down to calling them 'sir'.) He tried to point this out to us. He was once again told to go and get fucked.

An officer from our battalion appeared and joined the end of the queue. The journalist noticed his arrival and complained to the officer that men of his battalion had just told him to go and fuck off.

'Well you had better fuck off then,' replied the officer. We all laughed.

All in all our relationship with the press was a good one. This mainly came about because they were with us.

They faced the same threat, shared the same hardships. Mind you, they made loads more money than we did.

The only time I recall that we had any real bad feeling towards members of the British press was when we all saw the *Sun*'s 'Gotcha' headline, announcing to the world the sinking of the *General Belgrano* and the loss of over 300 lives. If one of us had shouted 'Gotcha' after the Belgrano was sunk then to us, that was okay, because we were there, we were putting our lives on the line and by our reckoning that gave us a right to say and think as we pleased. But a person 8,000 miles away from the war has no right to write such a thing, because they are risking nothing.

To us, such comments were insulting. They made light of the war we found ourselves involved in. Believe me. There's nothing light about war.

Generally idiotic questions
(Fitzroy)

I was wet, cold and miserable. As I looked out from my trench the first snows began to fall. Almost in unison a chorus of voices called out from the surrounding trenches, cursing the climate. This was all we needed, snow. I sank back down to the bottom of my hole and consciously made the decision to have a few moments of self-pity. If life's a piece of shit, when you look at it, just for a while, give in to it – it can help.

As I sat in my hole, drinking yet another mug of tea,

the air filled with the sound of an approaching helicopter. The noise from the machine's engine told me that it was not passing, but circling our position. Still holding my tea, I poked my head above ground level to see who or what was arriving. The helicopter landed and three men jumped out, a general, the general's adjutant and a radio operator. A sergeant called out from the trench next to mine:

'Well, fuck me. If it isn't one of our glorious leaders. I wonder what the fuck this mentally retarded wanker wants.'

'Probably looking for the officers' fucking mess,' came a reply.

'Is that officers' fucking mess as in "*Galahad*, burnt Taffys", or officers' fucking mess as in "Pass the port, please, Rupert"?'

We all laughed. I still laugh at this, although sometimes I do try not to.

The three men passed from trench to trench, stopping briefly at each one to talk to the occupants. I slid back to the bottom of my hole and prayed they would not stop at mine. They did. I looked up towards the sky. Two of the men, the general and his adjutant, were looking down on me. I began to stand, to salute the general, but he waved me to stay as I was and asked me my name. I replied with my rank, name and unit.

The general then asked if I liked the Falkland Islands and was I enjoying it here? I've been asked a few stupid questions in my time, but this was Number One, it really took the biscuit. The sergeant had been psychic – he really was a mentally retarded wanker. My mind pieced together a suitable reply before my lips did.

'Well, sir, I'm 8,000 miles from home, in a place that has already proved itself to be the arsehole of the earth. Four of my friends are dead, I'm up to my neck in shit, mud and water, the killing is still going on and just to

128

top it off really nicely it's started to snow. How the fuck do you think I feel, shit for brains?'

My intelligence took hold . . .

My mind replayed some time from the past. I was in the cookhouse of an Army camp in Northern Ireland. I had just returned from a three-day border patrol and was trying to relax and write a few letters home. A sergeant entered the cookhouse; he looked around, took focus on me and asked what I was doing. Nothing in particular, I replied, and because I had just returned from a patrol wanted to keep it that way. He told me that I was to report to the signaller in the operations room, where I would be given further instructions. I called the sergeant a shithead, behind his back, put my writing materials away and made my way to the operations room.

On reaching the ops room I reported, as per my instructions, to the corporal in charge. He explained that at any time now, a general was going to arrive. The ops room was undermanned and I was to operate the cameras during his visit. There were two television cameras on the top of telegraph poles in the High Street of Forkhill; both cameras could be operated by remote control from the ops room. The general, with his entourage in tow, entered the ops room and began to talk to the CPL in charge.

He then came and stood by me. I continued to stare at the two television monitors and at the same time zoomed the cameras in and out and tried to give the impression that I was dedicated to the task in hand. The general then spoke.

He said, 'Gosh, this all looks a bit complicated, it must be a bit like operating a nuclear submarine.'

'I wouldn't know, sir,' I replied, 'I've never operated a nuclear submarine.'

The general gave me a look that said, 'I suppose I left myself open for that one,' told me to carry on doing a good job and with entourage once more in tow he left the room. As the Regimental Sergeant-Major passed the back of my chair, he dug me in the small of the back with his pace stick, then whispered in my ear that he would see me later. I had only been with the battalion for a month, I was terrified. The next day, the RSM caught up with me. He explained the errors of my ways and then sent me off to the cookhouse to wash dishes and peel vegetables. He told me that this would give me ample time to digest his words of wisdom.

I returned to my trench in the Falklands. I once again felt the pain of my old RSM's pace stick in the base of my back. I once again recalled the hours that I had spent peeling vegetables. I looked up at the general and told him I was fine, really enjoying myself, and that I felt honoured to be here on the Islands serving my country.

He said, 'Well done,' congratulated me on the construction of my trench, and off he went.

As the general's helicopter finally lifted off and disappeared over the horizon, the sergeant next door called out his final comment: 'And where the fuck's the Argentine Air Force when you need the bastards?'

Once again laughter broke out around the trenches. I was still wet and I was still cold, but thanks to the general's visit I was no longer miserable. The general's visit to boost the troops' morale had worked.

I have often wondered if the joke was maybe on me. That maybe, as the general's helicopter had lifted into the air, he didn't turn to his adjutant and say: 'Did you see the look on that para's face when I asked him if he was enjoying it here? Ha, ha!'

We live and, hopefully, we learn . . .

Laugh . . . we nearly paid his Access bill
(Fitzroy)

Once again we were dug in. A pay corps corporal arrived at our location and began to hand out mail. I received a letter from my wife, Kathy, and settled into the bottom of my hole and began to read. Halfway through my letter I heard a loud laugh coming from the trench next to mine. The laughter grew louder and louder and I looked out of my trench to see what was so funny.

Yank, who was in the hole next door climbed from his trench and called aloud: 'Come and listen to this fucker!'

Everyone else had heard his outburst and soon an audience had assembled around his trench. Yank climbed on to a peat wall he had built and began by explaining that he had just had the pleasure of receiving a letter from the credit card company, Access. He then began to read the letter aloud: 'Dear Lance-Corporal Thayer, According to our records your account is in arrears to the amount of £243.'

'You naughty boy,' said someone in the assembled crowd, which was followed by more mock calls of disapproval and the suggestion that they should bring back hanging for the likes of him. Yank held out his hand so that it could be slapped.

He continued: 'If full payment is not received by us within seven days of the above date then we shall commence legal proceedings against you.'

The air filled with tut-tuts. Yank stopped reading and said: 'Well men, it looks like I'm going to court.'

I asked if I could come along with him. Someone else said that he wouldn't mind a trip to the courts and didn't they have a coffee-machine there? Yank screwed the letter up and threw it in the mud. At the same time, and with a voice that was filled with deep concern, he said: 'You know something guys? I'm really fucking worried.'

I nearly died. I fell to my knees and couldn't stop myself laughing for the rest of the day. I know that I, and I am sure that everyone else who had heard the corporal read his letter that day, would have loved to have been back in England, in court and facing the horrors of owing money to Access.

Since that day I have received such letters from the machines that write them. I read them, screw them up and then search for a piece of mud to throw them in. I say: 'I'm really fucking worried.'

No one laughs.

Little cold toes on little cold feet
(Wireless Ridge)

As the light of day began to fade we moved round and dug into the base of Mount Longdon. Our sleeping-bags were in our packs. The packs hadn't caught up. It would be another cold night.

During the previous hours of darkness, our sister battalion, 3 Para, had assaulted and captured Mount Longdon. It had taken them many hours; it had cost them many lives. As we sat at the base of Mount Longdon it was still costing and they were still paying.

Having now lost the mountain, the Argentines were

throwing everything they had at its peak. Every few minutes a barrage of shells could be seen exploding on Longdon's summit. In between the barrages of shells there were barrages from a multi-barrel rocket launcher. After the noise of impact white clouds of smoke puffed into the air and blew sideways, carried by the wind.

After every barrage a machine-gun could be heard opening up from the top of Mount Longdon. The bullets coming from the gun's barrel said this: 'Hello, we're 3 Para, and we're still fucking here'.

The defiant 3 Para gunner on the top of Mount Longdon became our hero. Go on, we said. You fucking show them, mate. You show them that no matter what they hit you with you will always be there, they will never drive you back, they can only pull you forward.

Up until that point I had always dug in with Jed and Frank had always dug in with Yank. For some reason, which according to Frank was Yank's fault and according to Yank was Frank's, Frank and Yank had had a fall out. Frank had then 'sacked' Yank from his position of company storeman. We had tried to point out to Frank that he couldn't go around sacking people. This was the Army. Getting the sack was something that just doesn't happen in the Army. Frank replied that it was his store and he'd sack who the fuck he liked. Yank said he couldn't give a fuck about being sacked because he wanted to go back to the Mortar Platoon where he belonged.

We then spent the rest of the daylight hours having to listen to Frank bitching about Yank and Yank bitching about Frank. I swear, the way they were going on you would have thought they were married.

Eventually darkness fell and Jed, ever the diplomat, informed me that I was to go and sleep with Frank and that he would sleep with Yank. When we finally decided that despite the cold we must try to get some sleep, Frank and I, both wrapped in everything we had, lay pressed against each other in the bottom of our trench. It was a very cold night. It was also a very beautiful night. Lying on my back, looking skywards, the darkness and the thousands of shining stars upon it surrounded everything. The ground, the rocks, our equipment and our clothing were covered with a white frost. The stars illuminated the frost, everything appeared white and bright.

As we lay, trying to sleep, Frank began to complain that he couldn't feel his feet. Frank then became scared. Very scared. His fear had nothing to do with thoughts of death, war and Argentines, he was scared that the oncoming frostbite in his feet would cause him to be 'casevaced'. Frostbitten feet and feet with trench foot had put more British soldiers out of the fighting than any other thing – including deaths and injuries in battle. Since we had landed on the Islands Frank had spent any spare time he found himself with running around the company threatening all and sundry with instant death should anyone go down with trench foot or frostbite. He said that these conditions were brought about by bad soldiering. In fact this was not true and Frank knew it. But no doubt because of his words soldiers did take extra care of their feet. In fact our company did not lose one man through trench foot or frostbite, which considering that most of our men carried far heavier weight than the men of rifle companies, i.e. mortar and anti-tank equipment, was no small achievement.

Now in a trench one mile and one day away from victory, Frank's feet were succumbing to the cold. We had been taught in training that the warmest part on a human body is the crotch area and the second warmest is under the armpits. Frostbitten feet should be placed on these areas. Colour-sergeant or not, there was no way that I was going to allow Frank to wrap his feet around my balls so we settled for the armpits. I sat between his legs, zipped open my clothing and Frank stuck his two feet in, one under each arm.

They really were cold. After a while Frank's circulation returned, he could feel his feet again and he stopped being scared.

Since that day, whenever I see Frank and he breaks into his impression of me at Goose Green after I was caught in the Blowpipe's backblast, i.e. he puts on a child's voice and says: 'I've been hit! I've been hit!' I always reply: 'Oh my feet, oh my poor feet. Help me, Luke.'

Then we both laugh.

Why not? I'm still breathing and he's still got feet.

When I need you
(Wireless Ridge)

It was night. We were dug in close to our mortar line. It was a quiet mortar line. A waiting mortar line. Through the darkness came the constant sounds of artillery. Some theirs. Most ours.

I was in a slit trench with Frank. As I zipped myself into my sleeping-bag I felt grateful for its presence. The world was not such a bad place. I had my doss bag, I was going to get some proper sleep. The two previous nights had been the coldest so far; we hadn't had our bergens, they hadn't caught up. No bergens – no doss-bags; no doss-bags – no sleep.

I pulled my sleeping-bag over my head and at the

same time pushed my body down inside so that the bag completely covered me and the warm air that I breathed out remained within the bag. I put my right hand into my left armpit, I drew my knees up to my chest and put my left hand between my legs. This was the position that I always found myself going off to sleep in on the Islands. It is also the position I always find myself going off to sleep in today.

The Argentine shelling increased, although most of it was landing quite a distance away from us. Then one barrage landed close. Very close. With every explosion I found myself flinching. Frank, who was lying beside me, had a go at me for my flinching – he said my nervousness was making him nervous. I asked was he sure it was me? Was he sure that the exploding shells had nothing to do with it?

Our silent mortar line opened fire. I couldn't believe the noise. It pierced my brain. It left my ears and my head physically hurting. I had never been that close to a firing mortar line before and as I was a good fifty yards away from it I wondered how it felt for the mortar crews who were stood right on it. I had the thought that they were sure to be very deaf in later years.

Eventually the firing stopped. My ears still rang but I was able to fall into sleep.

Then I awoke. Frank was still sleeping. I crawled out of my doss bag and out of our trench. Outside the morning was beautiful. It was very bright, everything appeared very clear, very sharp. It was also warm. I stretched out my arms and let out a deep yawn. I then walked up the hill we were dug in against. On the top of the hill was a large plateau that stretched as far as the eye could see in all directions. I turned to my right and began to walk in the direction we had come from the day before, away from Port Stanley. In the distance the sounds of battle began to grow. Distant explosions, distant booms and bangs. Just a few at first, then more, then louder.

As I walked I passed a group of running British soldiers. They were all dressed in World War II uniforms, they wore metal helmets and carried old .303 rifles with bayonets attached. As they ran past me towards the distant sounds of battle, I smiled at them: they in turn smiled at me.

I continued to walk and passed another British soldier. The bottom part of his left leg was missing. The stump was bleeding. He was on the ground, sitting up, leaning back slightly and supporting his weight on his arms, which were stretched out behind him. At the same time he was trying to lift his stump so that he could look at it. I had seen the soldier before, in Fitzroy, he had been on the *Galahad*, that was where he had lost his leg. As I passed him I said nothing, I just smiled. He smiled back at me, shrugged his shoulders, pointed at his stump and said, 'Cor blimey, eh?'

I waved goodbye to the legless soldier and continued walking back. I passed a British artillery line. The guns were firing. All the soldiers were busy loading and firing; at the same time they were all singing. It resembled a scene from *Oh What a Lovely War*. I once again waved at the soldiers I passed. Once again the soldiers I passed waved back at me.

I continued to walk. I passed a church service. The padre was standing on a box. He was leading his congregation in the hymn 'Onward Christian Soldiers'. The padre noticed me pass. He waved for me to join them. I smiled at him, shook my head and continued to walk.

The noises of battle began to fade into silence. The silence then began to fill with the sound of the wind. Quiet at first, growing louder. As the sound of the wind grew, the brightness of the day began to fade. A mist fell, wrapping itself around me, around everything. I came to a tarmac road. I stopped. The road was perfectly straight and disappeared into the horizon to my left and the horizon to my right.

I crossed the road, the wind fell silent, the mist lifted, the sun shone again, birds sang. In front of me was an old stone farmhouse. I walked around the building and entered through the back door and into a kitchen. In the kitchen was a sink. At the sink was my mother. She turned and noticed me. She said I was late. Where had I been? She walked up to me and asked what the muck on my face was. I explained that it wasn't muck, it was camouflage cream. She told me to wash it off and to never come home so dirty again. I said I was sorry, but I had been to war; I had to look like this.

In the corner of the kitchen was a large table, with benches running along its two longest sides. I made towards the table and sat down. I was tired. I put my face into my hands and pulled the sleep from my eyes with my fingers.

I looked up from my hands. I had been joined at the table. Sat opposite me were my two sisters, Faith and Micky. Next to them sat my sister-in-law, Margaret, whom I had once shared a house with when I was seventeen. On my right was Jean, the first woman I made love with. On my left sat Shelly, the first woman I lived with.

A bowl of stew appeared on the table in front of me. I looked to see who had brought it – it was Kathy. She smiled, leant over and softly kissed me on the cheek.

As I ate my stew I looked at the women who surrounded me. Their presence was calming. It was as though they were stroking my mind, calming my body, easing my existence and yet not touching me.

I got up from the table and kissed each of them in turn. I went over to the sink where my mother still stood. I explained I had to go back to the battle. I kissed her on the cheek. I turned away and opened the back door. As I stepped out of the house, I felt a hand on my shoulder. I

138

turned and saw my Aunt Letty. She smiled at me and at the same time wrapped a scarf around my neck and tucked it into my jacket. She told me: be careful, take no risks, be clever. Then she kissed me.

I walked out of the house and back across the tarmac road. The sun disappeared again. The birds stopped singing. The sound of the wind began to rise, mist began to fall.

I heard a shell whistling in. I looked to the sky and saw a mortar round falling. It was falling in slow motion. It fell to the ground in front of me. I watched as gravity very slowly pushed it into the soil.

It exploded. I awoke.

In my mind today I recall that dream as well as I do any of the real events I walked through on the Islands. It also left me with many questions. One day I must try to answer them.

Incoming spoons
(Wireless Ridge)

Snow was falling. The morning was freezing. I stood outside my trench, jumping up and down on the spot in an attempt to keep warm. In the valley below, soldiers of my battalion had organised a game of British Bulldog. It had started as a friendly 'Touch' bulldog game and as with all things 'Airborne' had progressed into an all-out brawl. An officer called a halt to the proceedings before – as he put it – they did more damage to themselves than the Argentines could ever hope to inflict upon them. The boys stopped playing, got a bit of a dog on and returned to their trenches on the slope.

At one point two soldiers came running back down off the slope and into the valley. It was apparent that they were racing each other to the other side and back. On their return leg the valley came under artillery fire. As the first shell impacted into the valley floor the two soldiers threw themselves to the ground. Once the shelling had apparently stopped, they got to their feet and carried on running back towards the slope. More shells landed. They dived to the floor again. For some reason the spectacle of watching the two soldiers attempt to get back across the valley in one piece was one of the funniest things I had ever seen. I was not alone: everyone else on the slope unanimously burst into laughter.

Eventually, to rousing applause from us on the slope, the two soldiers made it safely back to their trenches and, with a smile on my face, I turned back to the job I had in hand. On the ground in front of me was my cooker on which I was heating water in a mess tin.

I was going to have some oatmeal with drinking chocolate for brekkie.

The water boiled and I poured it into my black plastic mug. I then stirred in the drinking chocolate sachet and added a crumbled oatmeal block.

As I stood outside my hole, eating my breakfast, I thought that life was not that bad. We had had our sleeping-bags the previous night and so I had slept well and felt refreshed. We had also been resupplied with food and water and now that I was putting something warm into my body I wasn't too bothered about the cold.

Halfway through my meal I dropped my spoon. The spoon landed on top of the peat bank that I had constructed around my trench. As I leant over to pick the spoon up it began to slide off the bank and into the trench. The bottom of the trench was covered with watery mud. I didn't want my spoon to land in the mud. I dived forward and caught it just before it reached the bottom.

Feeling happy with myself for having caught the spoon, I stood to my feet. Everyone around me was lying on the ground.

'Fuck,' I said, and dived to the ground. Obviously there was something incoming that I had not heard. I lay on the ground awaiting an explosion. None came. I looked up from the ground and to the other soldiers who were still lying around me.

The inquest began.

'What did you fucking dive for? What did you hear?' asked a sergeant from the Anti-Tank Platoon in the direction of Yank.

'I didn't hear nothing. I dived because Frank fucking dived,' replied Yank.

The inquest turned to Frank.

'I fucking dived because Luke fucking dived,' said Frank.

I wondered if I should start running straight away or at least try to explain that I hadn't dived, I was just picking up my spoon.

When I did explain about the dropping of my spoon everyone fell to the ground in laughter with the main barrage of comments being directed towards Frank.

I was lucky though. Without a doubt Colour-Sergeant Frank Pye could out-punch me. But there was no way that he could ever out-run me.

I won the fight by at least a hundred yards.

Once The Pye had calmed down I crept back slowly to our position and thankfully, for me, by that time he was also seeing the funny side of the spoon incident.

Out of nowhere a Harrier came screaming up the valley from the direction of Port Stanley. A few seconds later three Argentine Skyhawks followed in hot pursuit. Because we were dug in halfway up one of the valley slopes the planes flew past us at almost eye level. They came and went in seconds.

A short period of time later one Skyhawk, which had obviously been hit, because it was smoking, came screaming back down the valley. This time it had the Harrier on its tail. The other two Skyhawks were never seen again.

Later that same morning I sat near my trench drinking a cup of tea. Suddenly there was a loud, explosive noise. Once again I instantly felt fear and dived to the ground. This time it was everyone's turn to laugh at my expense.

The loud explosion that I heard had been caused by a Scorpion tank test-firing its weapon. The tank was parked no more than twenty metres from my trench, but for some reason I had failed to notice its arrival. When the tank fired its guns, and I panicked, the cause of my panic was not the loudness of the noise of the explosion, but that it was a new noise. A noise of war that I had not heard before.

In war there are many noises, in fact, war is without a doubt a very noisy affair. As time went by I found myself becoming familiar with the sounds of battle. I was able to say 'that's one of our mortars' or 'that's one of theirs', etc. On hearing any new noise, my mind automatically conjured up images of some secret Argentine weapon that I had not heard of before.

Today, more than anything, it's noises that take me back to the battlefields of the Falklands. A passing jet can do it. A sudden clap of thunder. But mostly, it's the unexpected, the unfamiliar sounds.

Sometimes, just for a second or two, I wish I was deaf.

To walk with ignorance is to walk in bliss (Wireless Ridge)

Something was different. I think we all sensed it before we were told. The air was quieter: not so much shooting in the distance, not such a heavy smell of fear. Someone – with a radio – said it looked like they were about to jack.

This was good news. Very good news. We waited to hear more.

In the distance, maybe half a mile away, two soldiers walked across the landscape. As we sat around, some of us looking to the ground, some of us smoking, some talking, all waiting, someone who was examining a map exclaimed aloud: 'I think those two stupid fucking hats over there are walking through a minefield.'

We all looked up. This could be interesting.

'I'll have two quid on the little fucker gettin' it first.'

We all laughed.

At the same time we all jumped to our feet and began to shout and wave at the two soldiers in an attempt to warn them. They both stopped and began to look around to discover who was shouting and why. They noticed us. We all began waving and shouting again: 'You're in a fucking minefield.'

They both waved back and then continued walking.

We couldn't help but laugh. They had obviously thought that we paratroopers were waving 'Hello' to them. We loved these two. They really were stupid fucking hats.

'Do any of you fuckers want my two quid before it's too late?'

Then to my amazement I heard these words: 'Luko-wiak, run over there and warn 'em.'

I looked around to see who was talking. It was the new adjutant. I didn't want to go. But here's a funny thing: I do believe that I actually took almost a whole pace forward before I realised it. I stared in disbelief at the adjutant.

He looked at me, smiled and then broke out laughing. Everyone else also laughed. Then I laughed.

Eventually, after quite a deep philosophical debate, the conclusion was drawn that the two soldiers walking through the minefield, were, at the end of the day, far better off not knowing what they were walking through. They were already in the middle of it. They had to walk out of it – which was what they were already doing – so why go making things more difficult for them by giving them knowledge of the mines around them?

'You got a point. But let's tell the fuckers anyway.' Once again we all laughed.

We didn't hear any bangs, so we presumed that they made it.

The above story is one that is frequently remembered whenever I meet the others who were there that day. The great unanswered question always remains; was the adjutant really joking when he told me to go and warn the two soldiers in the minefield or did it dawn on him just how stupid a thing it was to say after he had said it? I always say: 'Who knows? Who cares? All's well that ends well.'

Then I go for a walk.

Headless, legless, lifeless smokers
(Wireless Ridge)

Happy or what? – I should co-co.

They have jacked. Argentines are streaming off the mountains and back down into Port Stanley. Rumour Control says they want to talk. They know they can't possibly win.

The order was given to 'Make Safe'.

We made safe our weapons by taking out the round we had 'up the spout' and applying our safety catches. We hoped they would stay that way.

Jed produced a plastic Union Jack and a small hip flash of whisky from his equipment. The Union Jack was placed on top of a bergen and the hip flask was passed between us. A toast was made. At the time I may have believed that we were toasting victory. Today, I know we were toasting life.

We grouped around a clump of rocks and a photograph was taken. In the photograph I am in the bottom left-hand corner, squatting on the ground. In my right hand I hold a Benson & Hedges King Size cigarette and on my face I hold the truest of smiles. I was very happy.

I have seen the same photograph a hundred times in a hundred different books. There's always a clump of rocks. There's always a group of men. Dressed the same, holding guns. There's nearly always a Union Jack and the group of men always have smiling faces.

There are never any dead men.

If these words are ever published, then I would like the photograph of me and my rocks, group of men, Union Jack, smiling faces and no dead men to be printed in colour and take up a whole page – maybe even two. Underneath it, I would write these words: 'Happy or what? I should co-co'.

After the taking of the photograph – to really celebrate – I said to myself: 'Let's have a cup of drinking chocolate.' Then I smiled.

I found a nice space in between the rocks and took my webbing from my back. I then took my mess tins from my webbing and from my mess tins I took my plastic bag of drinks. From my plastic bag of drinks I took my last sachet of drinking chocolate and from my last sachet of drinking chocolate I took the powder it contained. Then I took my cooker from my webbing and from my cooker I took my box of hexie tabs. From my box of hexie tabs I took two square white fuel tablets. Then I took a water bottle from my webbing and from the top of the water bottle I took my black plastic cup. Then I had another smile. With some matches that I took from my smock I lit the square white fuel tablets and then put the square white fuel tablets onto the cooker. Then on to the cooker I put a mess tin and in the mess tin I put some water.

Every now and then, as I watched my water boil, I jumped to my feet and did a little jig of joy. On one of my jigs, the last to be exact,

I time flashed . . .

I didn't know where I was. I didn't know how old I was or even who I was. But I could see. I could see a black and white moving image of a small man who had a small black moustache. His name was Hitler. He was doing a 'Jig for Joy'.

Why not? France had just fallen.

I returned to Wireless Ridge. I stopped jigging. I sat back down.

I was still very happy though. I can remember a group of soldiers passing to my rear. I could hear them shouting aloud, 'Well done, 2 Para.' They were from our sister battalion, 3 Para. (Come to think of it seems strange to me now that battalions in the British Army refer to each other as 'sisters'.) I jumped to my feet and shouted, 'Well done, 3 Para.'

I can also recall singing aloud the Queen song, 'We are the Champions'. It summed it up. We were the champions.

Sometimes, I try so hard to relive those moments on Wireless Ridge. I was so happy. There was no pain. No anger. No hate. No quarrels. No work. No bills. No women. No sex.

I felt I was the human being that creation had meant me to be. The man I had read about in the Old Testament, the one who had once walked naked, in paradise. Always happy. With no questions to ask. No lies to be told. I was original man. I was Adam.

Someone called my name: 'Hey, Luke. You have to see these two poor fuckers.'

I finished drinking my chocolate and put my black plastic cup back onto my water bottle. Then I put my water bottle back into my webbing and put my plastic bag of drinks into my mess tins. Then I . . . only joking!

I put everything away and followed my friend up a path which ran along the edge of the ridge. At the end of our climb we reached a plateau. Department store dummies no longer entered my mind. Dead men no longer entered my mind. I passed the Argentine casualties of war without a thought for their lack of life. I was now blind to it. I felt nothing.

We found the two I had to see.

They were lying on their backs, shoulder to shoulder. One of them had no head, the other no legs. The head and the legs had been blown off in such a way that they could have been removed by surgeons. I have a friend who has a photograph of the headless, legless Argentines that lay motionless on the plateau of Wireless Ridge. It measures nine inches by five and is in black and white. He keeps it in a photograph album. Underneath the

147

photograph he has written these words: 'Heads I win, Tails you lose'.

The boy with no head and his friend with no legs became celebrities amongst the soldiers of my battalion. The photograph my friend has in his album was not one that he had taken himself. It had been taken by our official battalion photographer. After the war, in the safety of Aldershot, we could, if we so wished, purchase a copy of the 'Heads I win, Tails you lose' Argentines. I did not purchase a copy. I had no wish to own such sick memorabilia.

Two days after the battalion photographer had pointed his camera at the boy with no head and his friend with no legs he was accidentally shot through the side of his face by a friend of his who was examining an Argentine Colt .45 pistol. Some friend. He was very lucky. He lived.

I took no photographs during my time on the Falkland Islands. I held more respect for war than that.

We left the headless, legless Argentines and made our way around the position of trenches they had lost their lives defending. There were many other twisted corpses scattered around, littering the ground. Once again we were struck by how young most of them appeared. By this time we had become reasonably proficient at diagnosing cause of death and as we inspected various dead people we drew the conclusion that none of them had died from gunshot wounds – they had all been killed by artillery fire. The conscripts' fear and inexperience had pulled them from their holes, when their best bet would have been to stay put. This was of course easy for us to say – but not so easy for them to do.

In one of the trenches there was a dirty green blanket – it moved. Yank and I both jumped back and at the same time cocked our weapons. Out from under the blanket appeared an Argentine soldier. He had not noticed our presence. He got to his feet, stretched out his arms and let out a big yawn. He had obviously just woken up. He finished yawning, opened his eyes and finally noticed us.

'Hello,' I said.

Seems ridiculous now, but that is what I said. Yank said that the Royal Artillery were going to be well pissed off with this one should they ever find out that he had slept through their biggest artillery barrage since Korea.

With our machine-guns, we gestured for the Argentine to climb from his trench. Yank covered him with his weapon and I gave him a quick body search. As I searched him I told our prisoner that the war was over. 'The war. Finito,' I said.

On hearing this the Argentine smiled. Why not? He was still alive.

The Argentine had three stripes on the breast pocket of his jacket. He was a sergeant. When I had finished searching him he made the gesture of smoking a cigarette with one of his hands. I turned to Yank and said you had to admire the front of this one. We've only known him a few minutes and he's bumming fags already. Yank replied that he was a fucking sergeant all right; just like our wankers, always on the fucking bum for things. We both laughed. The Argentine also laughed. I gave our new prisoner a Benson & Hedges King Size and a light to go with it and he thanked us for our kindness.

Across the plateau we saw a line of Argentine prisoners being marched away to a holding area. Yank said he would escort our prisoner over to the others and that he would see me later.

I should have gone with Yank.

One Less to Feed Thanks to Me
(Wireless Ridge)

Yank took the prisoner away. I carried on walking amongst the Argentine trenches. Although I was surrounded by death, I was still happy, I can recall singing aloud the words to a song I know.

The song talks of dreaming and dying and a soul leaving its body unexpectedly.

I came across another trench and jumped in. I searched amongst the left-behind equipment that lay scattered about the floor. There was nothing I was particularly looking for. I was just looking for looking's sake. I found a discarded wrapper from an Argentine packet of sweets. For some reason wrappers with Argentine writing and the Argentine manufacturers' names and addresses held a fascination for me. I would look at them and say to myself, 'See – they have sweets and they have factories that make the sweets, and people who work in the factories.' Why these things were of such great interest to me I do not know. Maybe, in times of war, confirming the obvious is something that we just find ourselves doing.

I had had enough of the hole I was in and climbed out in search of another.

I had the thought that the factories that make the sweets are probably surrounded by towns, in which the people who work in the factories live in houses.

I looked across the plateau and saw another trench. I approached it from the side. Crouched in the trench was a figure in grey. I saw him. He saw me. He held a rifle. I moved the first finger on my right hand. Bullets left the end of my machine-gun. They hit the figure in grey. They impacted into his chest and threw him back against the side of the trench. Grey turned to red. He slid to the ground. His soul left him unexpectedly.

I sensed movement to my right. I heard voices shouting. I turned and at the same time crouched to the ground. Across the plateau, scurrying between the rocks, were three soldiers. They were all wearing red berets. I automatically thought that they had to be from 3 Para, there was nothing about the three soldiers that I recognised. I shouted out, 'It's all right, it's all right. I'm 2 Para.'

The three soldiers slowed to a walk. As they approached, one of them asked what the firing had been. I explained that one of the Argies had still been alive. I had come across him in his trench, he had a gun, I shot him.

'Oh well,' said one of the soldiers, 'one less of the fuckers to feed.'

I said my farewells to the three soldiers and made my way down off the ridge and back to where I had left my equipment. By the time I returned everyone else had already left.

Later, in Port Stanley, when I eventually caught up with Jed and Co, I said nothing of the life I had taken on Wireless Ridge. I don't know why I didn't tell anyone. It took me eight years to speak of it and even then, when I did, I lied.

A girlfriend had left me. A day came when I went to her and pleaded for her to return. In an attempt to win her back I tried for the first time to give some explanation for my behaviour. In the explanation of my life I spoke of the man I had shot on Wireless Ridge. In an attempt to win some sympathy from her, I said that after I had shot the figure in grey I jumped into the trench with him and grabbed his dead body. I said that I shook his corpse. That I shouted at him. That I was angry that he had been there. That I was angry that I had killed him.

I did not jump into the trench with the dead Argentine. I did not grab his clothing, shake his lifeless body or shout at him. I was also not angry. I sometimes like to believe that this was because I had no time to be.

As soon as I saw movement and heard shouting, I instantly thought of me. I worried that my firing might be misinterpreted by the approaching soldiers. I worried that they might start shooting at me. This was of course very selfish on my part, although I believe that it was also very human.

I lied to my girlfriend because I knew I could not explain why I had felt nothing, no remorse for the taking of another man's life. I knew I couldn't explain it to her because I was unable to even explain it to myself. I worried that the truth would make me sound heartless.

Today as I write these words I do feel sorrow that I killed a man on Wireless Ridge. In my mind I have played over the event many times. Sometimes I pretend that he wasn't armed, that he surrendered to me and that I took him prisoner. Other times I like to imagine that instead of shooting him I shouted at him to drop his weapon. I do know that if Yank and I had not come across the other Argentine then my weapon would not have been cocked. Maybe this would have prevented me from taking a life. I don't know. On the other hand, it may have cost me mine. Again, I just don't know.

Today, ten years on with the war long gone, I am left with lots of don't knows. I don't understand the logic of the world that I live in. The only thing that I do know, and I really do know this, is that I have two sons. One who carries my blood and one who does not. Blood is not important. I never want my sons to have to go to war and I never want my sons to take another human life.

I don't want yours to either.

Snap
(Port Stanley)

Our first couple of hours in Port Stanley were spent on the streets. We were just hanging around, having a smoke, a talk, we could walk around a bit if we liked, but we kept off the grass – it might be mined. Although we were all still very happy the initial jubilation had begun to die down a little. A feeling of 'let's just get home now' began to prevail. It seemed as though nobody cared that much to give an order and even less to receive one.

As I stood on a street corner talking with Frank and two soldiers from 3 Para that he knew, I thought about how everything had so suddenly changed.

Just like that: snap.

The thought of sudden change was largely pushed into my mind by the walking past of three Argentine soldiers who were still carrying weapons. They nodded hellos as they passed – we nodded hellos back. Couple of hours ago we had been at the forefront of the campaign to make Argentines an endangered species and now here we were, leaning on a lamppost on a corner in Port Stanley, letting breathing Argentines go by.

Oh me, oh my.

I was unable to stop myself from thinking, 'It's a funny old world'. They were armed, we were armed and yet it never once entered any of our minds to start shooting at each other. It was over. Snap.

As I looked about the streets of Port Stanley, I tried to take photographs with my mind. I wanted to remember the scene that surrounded me. The buildings that bellowed large clouds of smoke, causing everything to be tinted with grey. The two dead Argentines lying in the street. The live Argentines walking on by. The soldiers sitting on the ground resting their backs against fences, eating chocolate, smoking cigarettes. Apart from the fact that the Argentines wore grey and we wore green, they looked very similar to us. They looked tired. They looked happy.

As I talked with Frank and his two friends I held in my hand a lit cigarette. One of the 3 Para soldiers tapped me on the arm and asked: 'Two's up on yer fag, mate.'

This was para-speak for: 'May I inhale some smoke from your cigarette before you extinguish it, my friend?'

I told him that he could have a whole one to himself if he liked. Apparently 3 Para had run out of cigarettes days before. We, on the other hand, were still oversupplied thanks to our little stay at Goose Green. I went over to my bergen and gave the 3 Para soldier a whole packet. Talk about make a man happy.

The two Argentines who lay dead on the street nearby were not happy men. One of them, who lay in the road, didn't have a visible mark upon him. The other, who lay on the pavement, had one side of his face missing. It wasn't really missing though, because it lay on the pavement next to the good bit of his face. Bits of it hung over the kerb. The bits dripped blood into a puddle. The puddle turned red.

I had my photograph taken with one of the dead men who lay on the street in Port Stanley. I say I had my photograph taken with him only because he was dead and so therefore was unable to choose to have his photograph taken with anyone. At the time we all presumed that the two dead Argentines had been killed by shellfire. They were lying in the street outside a house that had received a direct hit from one of our artillery shells.

Then one day someone showed me a photograph of one of the dead men. It was the one with half his face missing. He had obviously been hit in the head. But by what?

This question arises because in the photograph behind the dead man is a wooden fence. In the wooden fence are bullet holes from small-arms fire. In this part of town there was no actual fighting between British and Argentine forces. The war had been called to a halt a few hundred yards up the road. Even if there had been fighting that far into town the bullets that hit the fence would have to have been fired from a weapon that faced in from the sea and not from up the road, which was the direction from which I and the rest of the 'goodies' had advanced. One of the conclusions that can be reached from the photograph is that the Argentine had been 'head-jobbed' or 'topped' or executed. But by whom? It couldn't have been any of us, it was too far into town. The last British shots had been fired way back.

We wondered if he had been shot by his own side. This would be an outrageous thought if it were not for the fact that many Argentine accounts of the war tell of Argentine officers shooting their own men.

I also heard of Argentine officers shooting their own men from an Argentine journalist. He had interviewed many Argentine Falkland veterans and heard these stories from them. I said I still found these tales hard to believe. During my talk with the Argentine journalist I mentioned the conversation that I had held with my company major before our departure to the Falklands. I said how I had told the major that I believed the Argentine invasion of the Falklands would bring about the downfall of the British Government.

The Argentine journalist seemed genuinely surprised by my comments and asked if it was normal for soldiers in the British Army to discuss politics with their superior officers. I said, 'Of course, along with the weather, the price of beer and the size of the tits on Page Three.' He said that he couldn't imagine Argentine officers and soldiers ever discussing such things. I asked, 'What? Tits

155

and beer?' 'No,' he said. 'Politics.' I replied that I couldn't imagine British officers and soldiers shooting each other.

Maybe the Argentine soldier who lay in the street in Port Stanley with one side of his face missing was killed by shell-fire. I guess I will never know. Unfortunately, artillery shells have no way of knowing who they kill, they have no sense of them and us, or good and bad. The shell that may have killed the two Argentines who lay in the street definitely did kill two Falkland Islanders who were in the front room of the house on the moment of impact. The two people who were killed were old ladies. They were the only Falkland Islanders to lose their lives during the conflict. They were also the oldest and the only female loss of life.

The part of town that they lived and died in had been evacuated by the Argentine authorities. The two old ladies had been requested to move, for safety's sake, into the centre of town. They refused the Argentine request. When the shell came hurtling through their roof and into their front room it was all over for them. Just like that.

Two dead old ladies. Two dead Argentine boys.

Snap.

Things you never knew about war
(No. 59)

Considering what you're risking – the pay's crap.

'I've been had a few times in me time, well who hasn't,

but I tell yeh, the one about the money down south, they fuckin' bent me over and shoved it up me sideways. Rubber fuckin' dicked or what? I mean, it wasn't like it was just a rumour, like I heard it from some cunt down the NAAFI, I was hearing this fucker from the cunts in the pay office. Fucking corporals an' all. Time I fucking spent working it all out, how much it all came to so far, what I was goin' to spend it on – fuckin' load of bollocks that all turned out to be. And Frank, he went fuckin' mental when he found out it was a rubber dick. I told him, it's all right for you fuckin' colour men, you fuckers get enough as it is, what about us fucking Toms? Should 'ave kept me fuckin' trap shut, on he then goes about when he was a Tom and how they only earned seven fuckin' pound a fucking week. I told him, my heart pumps purple piss.

'Here's the really mental fuckin' thing, when we were on the boat goin' down and comin' back again, we were earnin' more fucking money than when we were on the Islands running around blowin' away the fuckin' Argies. I mean, you know, how the fuck do they work that fucker out?

'Listen to this. Do you know what the fuckers told us? They said that as we were soldiers it was a hardship for us to be put on a fuckin' boat. Therefore, they have to pay us a hardship allowance. That's what they called it, a fuckin' hardship allowance. Well what the fuck's hard about being on a fuckin' ship playing cards, getting pissed and wankin' over porno mags? Beats the fuck out of runnin' about with some fucker shootin' at you. Stupid cunts.

'So, you see, we knew what we were getting when we were on the fuckin' boat, so naturally we all presumed that we'd be on more when we got on to the Islands. Well yeh fuckin' would wouldn't yeh? So when it starts flying around that we're getting another £3 a day for being there, it's fuckin' believable. Like I said, even the fucking

157

pay corporals thought it was gen. When the truth finally broke, we was in Port Stanley, war's fuckin' over and they had had us all hook line and fuckin' sinker.

'Mind you, I complain, there were a couple blokes from one of the rifle companies went to war and earnt fuck all. On the way down they were catchin' some rays on the deck and the silly fuckers went and fell asleep. They got burnt to fuck. Next thing they know they're up before Jonesie on a self-inflicted wound charge and he goes and takes a month's pay off them. We all thought that was way over the fuckin' top, that one. It's all right for a fuckin' colonel, money they fuckin' make, but a Tom, you take a month's pay off him and it wipes you for years. Not to worry. We all chipped in and bought 'em a tube of suntan lotion.

'You want to talk petty though, we were dug in on Sussex Mountain, day fuckin' two, and this corporal from the pay corps comes round and asks if anyone needs any fags. So yeah, I'm a smoker, so I ask for some. Do you know what I had to fucking do to get them? I had to fucking sign for them so that the price could be deducted from my pay. And I'll tell yeh fuckin' what, first pay slip when I got back home and they deducted £2.50 for the fags they gave me when I was at war. Fucking typical that is. Here we are losing million-pound fuckin' battleships and the fuckers hit us Toms for the price of a couple of packets of fags. I'll tell you, don't you ever believe that we were fighting for those fuckers.

'And we weren't doin' it for the money either.'

Jesus loves you?
(Redruth/Port Stanley)

When I was twelve I walked with a friend along the high street of my home town in Cornwall. Our route took us past the local cinema. On the cinema's outer walls hung two large display cabinets. Inside the cabinets were a dozen or so colour film stills, taken from the two films that were showing inside. The two films were both X Certificate.

I can recall wondering, as I eyed the stills' teasing content, what secrets were held beyond my reach behind the large green doors. What type of moving pictures appeared on the screen that I was not permitted to see.

We left the front of the cinema and walked down an alley that ran along the building's right-hand side We passed one of the cinema's side exits. The door was ajar.

After a brief discussion, we stole the necessary amount of courage from our souls and entered the building. In front of us was a large flight of concrete stairs. We quietly climbed the stairs and on reaching the top opened the large swing door that led to the auditorium. Inside it was dark. The coast was also clear. Five seconds later we were seated in the back row of the circle. We were in – hee, hee.

The film that was showing was called *The Graduate*, and the thing that made my friend and I feel like the luckiest boys in town, was that there, on the screen, were real large big girls' titties. Hard on or what?

We stayed and watched the film twice. Unfortunately halfway through the second showing of the support film, Michael Caine in a war movie entitled *Play Dirty* (and they weren't lying either), we were spotted by the cinema manager and chased out the way we had come in. Didn't matter – we had seen an X film. Better still, we ensured that everyone else knew that we had seen an X film. We bragged for months.

Since that afternoon of well-spent youth in Redruth I have seen *The Graduate* more times than I can remember. Over the years I have been able to notice changes in my mind through my changing attitudes to the film.

To explain: when I first saw the film I was overjoyed at the fact that I had seen nude women. Another time I began to appreciate the soundtrack and bought my first Simon and Garfunkel record on leaving the cinema.

When I was sixteen I lost my virginity to, and had a secret affair with, a much older woman. She was my Mrs Robinson. I had always loved Mrs Robinson, she had always appeared a beautiful woman. Much later, after the war, after prison, I watched the film on late-night TV. I had just divorced from Kathy. I was sad. I was drunk. When the film reached the part where Mrs Robinson is doing everything in her power to keep Ben and her daughter apart, I found myself on my knees in front of the screen shouting aloud, 'Bitch, bitch, bitch.' I hated her.

My affections swung from Mrs Robinson to her daughter Elaine; Elaine became the way a woman should be.

I was twenty-three.

We were aboard a ship in Port Stanley. The war was over. The killing had stopped. We were on the ship to rest up, have a bath, eat some fresh food and unwind. At the end of the first day aboard I made my way along the ship's silent night corridors and found my bunk. For the first time in a long time, as I laid my head on a pillow, I was warm, well-fed, clean and happy. I was very happy.

As I closed my eyes to the darkness I thought of home.

I thought of Kathy. Soon I would be home. Soon I would be with Kathy. I fell into sleep.

Pain tore me awake.

I had a toothache. The worst toothache I have ever had. I got out of bed, left the cabin and went to the washrooms. In front of a mirror I opened my mouth wide. I poked the tooth. I pulled the tooth. I poked it again. The pain increased. I went back to the cabin and returned to bed. As I buried my head in the blankets I tried telling my mind it didn't hurt but I knew I was lying. I got out of bed again, found a box of matches, and returned to the washrooms. I split a match with my teeth and poked the aching tooth.

'Bastard.'

It made it worse. The pain made me fall to my knees. I pulled my mouth to a tap and swilled it with cold water.

'You fucking bastard.'

It made it even worse. I had run out of ideas. I gave up. I admitted defeat and sank back down to my knees. The increased pain brought tears to my eyes. I did not know what to do.

I turned on God. I told him he was a cunt. If I had been the fucker who had nailed him up, I would have cut his balls off and stuck them down his throat. This was unfair. I had just been through all that shit and this was my fucking night off. It was plain unfair.

Using the sink I pulled myself to my feet and made my way back to the cabin, bed and misery.

I couldn't sleep. The pain would not allow it. I tossed and turned and cursed quietly to myself. Yank's voice came from the darkness.

'Eh, Luke, what the fuck's the problem, you're keeping me awake, you cunt.'

'I've got a fucking toothache.'

'Well go and fucking get something for it.'

'From where?'

'From the end of my fucking dick, where the fuck do you think? From the ship's Medical fucking Officer.'

'Oh yeah, I'm really gonna wake an officer at two in the morning: "Excuse me, sir, but I've got fucking toothache".'

'Fuck him.'

'Oh yeah, fuck him. You fucking fuck him.'

'Listen, you've just come from war. You're a hero fucking paratrooper. He's just come from England. He's a hero fucking nothing. Go on, wake the wanker.'

'You sure he's just come from England?'

'I'll give you a chance. You, you cunt, are keeping me awake with your fucking whining. Now either you get out of fucking bed and go and see the MO or I shall get out of my fucking bed and give you something to really go and see him about. Go on. Wake the fucking Naval spastic.'

I know good advice when I hear it.

I left the cabin. On the wall at the end of the corridor hung a plan of the ship. I quickly located the colour square with MO written on it and made my way up through the decks towards it. My route took me through the bar in which we had all been drinking a few hours before. The bar's shutters were down, a few empty Harp lager cans lay scattered on the floor and tables, and a few orange plastic chairs lay tipped over. The three video monitors hissed out white noise. I walked across the bar, out the other side and up another flight of stairs. I located the door with 'MO' written on it. I knocked twice.

The door was opened by a sleepy-eyed man in a dressing-gown. I apologised for disturbing his sleep and explained about my toothache. He told me to wait, closed the door and then appeared again a few minutes later dressed in a tracksuit. We walked a couple of doors down from his cabin and entered his surgery. I couldn't believe my eyes – he had an actual dental chair, he was an actual dentist. Lucky or what?

I happily lay in the chair and he began to examine my tooth. Not long now I thought. One prick of the old needle and, hey presto, no more pain. I was to be disappointed. The doctor said he could see nothing wrong with my teeth.

He walked over to a cabinet, took out something that was right medical looking, and began to inspect my ears. Nothing wrong with them either. I didn't care, I just wanted an injection.

He told me I couldn't have an injection. He then gave me two pills, said that should I die during the night I was to be sure to come and see him at morning sick parade, and then he sent me on my way.

As I walked back along the corridor, still in pain, I had the thought that maybe all Parachute Regiment NCOs were psychic. Yank certainly was. The ship's MO really was a Naval spastic.

I headed back down through the ship. I once again entered the bar and crossed the dancefloor towards the door on the other side of the room. The bar's shutters were still down, the floor was still littered with cans, and the tipped-over chairs remained tipped. White noise continued to hiss from the video monitors. Halfway across the dancefloor the hissing suddenly stopped. The room fell silent. Then I heard music: the opening bars to 'The Sound of Silence'.

I turned to the nearest monitor. On the screen was Dustin Hoffman and the opening credits to *The Graduate*. I felt a chill far worse than the one when I saw my first dead friend. I waited for the moment when some great significance would dawn on me, the moment I would finally understand something I had not understood before. Again, nothing happened. My mind told me that the sailor who was on radio duty in the room where the video player was sure to have been kept was bored so he put on a film. That's all.

I pulled up the nearest chair, sat down and asked for

163

forgiveness from the someone or something that I could not understand for not understanding his ways. My toothache disappeared. And so, while the rest of my battalion slept below, I sat alone, at three o'clock in the morning, on a ship docked in Port Stanley harbour and once again watched *The Graduate*.

I tell people this story and they say it's coincidence, that's all. Just coincidence. 'Yes, I know,' I reply. But that is a lie.

We're coming home, we've done our time (Port Stanley)

We were in Port Stanley for ten days. I didn't know that. I had to look it up. I thought that sounded about right, but just to check, I phoned a few friends. They agreed with me. They said, 'That sounds about right.' I was happy they said that. There is a part of me that feels a little ashamed that I don't know how many days we spent in Port Stanley. I feel that I should. I feel that I should know these exact figures and dates out of respect for something. Maybe the dead. I don't know. All I have is memories. But in their way they are similar to my days because I can't count them. They come and go.

I remember the first night. The house we moved into. Just that feeling of being inside again. We could make as much light as we liked. Had all the windows blacked out nicely. We had water permanently boiling on a peat stove. Fags and food and rest and life. They was good times, some of those Port Stanley nights. 'Just Rejoice.'

Three of us got our heads down on a large double bed. We took our boots off. Big thing in life that can turn out to be, taking your boots off when you haven't in a while. I fell instantly to sleep.

I was woken in the morning by a young girl who had a cup of tea for me. It was a bit like 'Goldilocks' in reverse. The Falkland Islanders had returned to their homes for a bit of 'Who's been sleeping in my bed?' I went into the kitchen and most people were up. Still eating and drinking and talking. But quiet talk.

The next day I went out into the peat shed to fill a basket with peat, for the fire in the front room. While in the shed a jet flew over at low level. It turned out that it was one of our Harriers. There really was no need for that. I nearly shat myself. When I got back to the house everyone else had a comment or two to make on the shitheads in the jet.

One morning I recall sitting in the front room of our house in Port Stanley. There was a loud blast, sounded somewhere near. It turned out to be a 'one-off'. There were lots of these little 'one-offs'. First thing that always sprang into my mind was 'counter-attack'. Which of course it never ever was. But that's training for you.

The 'one-off' on this particular morning had been caused by a British soldier stepping on a mine which had lain buried on the racecourse. I heard he lost a leg or something. Stupid, silly war.

I remember the day we left Port Stanley. Funny, I don't recall packing my kit, or walking down to the jetty, or even saying goodbye to people (though I'm quite polite, so I probably did). I remember standing on the landing craft, we were waiting for it to move away from the jetty and take us back to the MV *Norland*. I remember looking at Port Stanley and thinking 'feel something time'. But I didn't feel a lot. I was happy to be leaving the Falklands,

I felt no affection towards them. But something important had happened to me there and for some reason I had the thought that, one day, it would be an achievement for me to return. Three days max.

As we waited on the landing craft, a Royal Marine commando assault craft (which is one of those rubber dinghy things with an outboard) pulled up alongside the jetty. It carried three marines. One of them jumped up from the dinghy, landed on the jetty and secured their craft with a rope. It was a good jump, and the boy knew his knots, so we gave him a round of applause. The other two marines then jumped from the craft, more applause from us, and the three of them swaggered off into the sunset. We whistled the tune from the film *The Good, the Bad and the Ugly*. I think the three marines thought that we were Argentines, because they only spoke sign language back.

Once they had rounded the bend at the end of the jetty, a soldier jumped from our craft, went over to the marines' dinghy, untied the rope, and threw it to someone at the back of our craft who tied it up.

As we pulled away from the jetty, the little rubber craft bopped along in the waves behind us. I remember thinking how nice it all was when there was no violence involved. Had 'em good.

As we motored out of the harbour I had the thought that I hadn't seen a penguin. Penguins were quite a symbol of the war. Think Falklands – think penguins. I wanted to see one. But I didn't get to. And I don't know a para who did. It's one of those funny things now, that if I ever see one of those choccie bars, with a penguin on, or a TV commercial for them, I always think of the penguins on the Falklands. But I didn't see any of them, so then I think about things that I did see.

Gullible, gallant, horrified heroes
(MV *Norland*)

We were gathered on the *Norland*'s top car deck. Colonel Chaundler once again wished to address the heroes of his command. As he waited in the wings for his cue from the RSM, the whispered conversations began:

'What the fuck's he want now?'

'Dunno, I was havin' a nice wank in the bog over some of my hot Danish porno lust, some cunt goes bang, bang on the door, and next thing I know I'm being told to get my fuckin' arse down here.'

'I'm starting to get well pissed off with havin' to listen to all these wankers goin' on about how fuckin' wonderful we all are. Just want to be left alone.'

The RSM called the battalion to attention. We snapped to attention. I had snapped to attention many times before. But never like that. I had never felt such a strong feeling of belonging. So totally welded to the ones who surrounded me. It really did feel different. It made me feel pride.

Pride in me. Pride in what I was a part of.

Colonel Chaundler entered, returned the RSM's salute, turned to face us and then gave the order to stand easy. We stood easy. He began to speak.

He had failed us. He was sorry. He had tried, he really had, but alas to no avail. He asked us to believe that not one phone in Whitehall had rung without him being on the end of it. He had spoken to every Parachute Regiment general that he could. All of them, without exception, had agreed with him, but there was nothing even they could do about it.

'What in fuck's name is he on about?'

'Be fucked if I know. From what I'm understanding he might as well be talking in fuckin' Swahili.'

The colonel said that he knew we would agree with him when he said that what had been done to us was unjust. He said that all he could now feel was bitterness. He was sure that we all felt bitter too. He apologised again, he repeated that there was nothing he could do. He really was truly sorry.

'Any idea?'

'Nope. Not a fucking clue. All I can come up with is that he didn't hand his morphine in like a good boy and he's happily trippin' away.'

The colonel finally got to the point. We would not now be sailing all of the way home. The *Norland* was required for other duties in the Falklands and so we would now disembark at Ascension Island and fly the remaining leg to England.

'I still ain't got a fuckin' clue what he's apologising for.'

'Me neither. So fucking what, whoopie shit – we're flying home. I couldn't give a toss.'

'That's not what I've fucking heard.'

'Why don't you fuck off and die you small-pricked wanker.'

'Small? You wouldn't fuckin' like it up your arse, pal.'

We in the back row all laughed. The colonel continued. Even though we would now be robbed of the welcoming home that we so rightly deserved, i.e. we would not all arrive home en masse but by plane-loads at two-hourly intervals, we should try and look on the bright side of things – at least we would arrive home six days earlier.

'Hold on a minute. Just fuckin' hold on a minute. Am I fuckin' getting this right? They want to cut six days off our journey home and that psychopathic bastard up there was trying to stop them?'

'I hadn't looked at it like that. You're fuckin' right,

168

must have been the war, he's fuckin' well shot away, he is.'

The colonel said that he did have one final avenue to try but he held little or no hope of achieving any success – but he would try. Try for us. His men.

We were horrified.

The last thing we wanted him to do was to go about adding days to our return. All we wanted was home and the sooner the better – to hell with the size of the reception.

'Let's assassinate the cunt, right away.'

'I'll tell you pal, the next time I see his fucking face, I want it to be in a snuff movie.'

'I told you. He's fuckin' well shot away.'

At the end of the day our colonel failed in his mission to keep us aboard the *Norland* and we did fly the remaining leg home from Ascension Island.

Today I own a videotape. I bought it for three quid from a car-boot sale in Exeter. The tape tells the story of the Falklands War. I have watched it many times, on my own and with others. I find that if I watch with others I am permanently pointing to the screen and saying, 'That's me,' or, 'I was there when they hit that.'

I find that I am able to sit and watch the moving colour images of the war I was witness to with little or no emotion. The images of the corpses at Goose Green I just accept. Even the pictures of the men I once knew being buried I just accept. I just accept everything. And why not? I'm still alive – what more can I do?

Then the tape reaches the part that shows our home-coming. As I see again the planes landing at Brize Norton and I watch the pictures of tearful families and grateful soldiers, my mood instantly changes. When I see again people rushing into each other's arms, fathers picking up children and happy face after happy face, I begin to cry. If I am with others I always race to turn the video off. I have no wish to show my emotions. Especially to myself.

Also shown on the tape are images of the ships coming home. One of the ships carried the Royal Marines – all of them. Their ship is surrounded by thousands of little boats. Tens of thousands of people wait for them on the quay. There is scene after scene of crying families, happy soldiers, bands loudly playing 'Rule Britannia.' As I watch the marines arrive I also begin to cry. I cry because it reminds me of my homecoming but I also cry because I feel we were robbed.

Please listen.

These are historical facts: my battalion, 2 Para, were the first battalion to land on the Islands. At Goose Green we were the first British unit into battle and we were the only British unit who fought two battles on the Islands. We were also the first British troops into Port Stanley. If anyone deserved a decent homecoming it was us.

But we didn't get one.

Sing if you're happy that way
(MV *Norland*)

I have read, and also seen, many accounts of the exploits of my battalion, 2 Para, when we were 'Down South' and they all, for some reason, fail to mention one of our war's leading characters. Someone whom all of us knew.

His name I do not know. I, like everyone else, only knew him by his nickname. His nickname was Wendy. Wendy was homosexual, he was an arse bandit, a turd burglar, a shirtlifter, a dirty fucking queer, a stinking poof, a fucking homo (I have to stop there – I can't remember any more stones).

He was also a good man.

Wendy worked as a steward aboard the MV *Norland*. On our journey to the Falkland Islands the ship stopped at Freetown in Sierra Leone to take on supplies. While there, the *Norland*'s civilian crew were given the option to either stay aboard and go to war or disembark and go back to England.

Wendy chose to stay.

The first time that I saw Wendy was on the evening of our first day aboard. I was waiting, along with many others, for the duty-free shop aboard the *Norland* to open. I was sat on the floor with my back resting against the shop's closed shutters, listening through my left ear to the band Supertramp who were playing on my Walkman.

Supertramp sounded like this: 'Dreamer, you're nothing but a dreamer.'

Through my right ear I was listening to a Lance-Corporal from one of the rifle companies, who in fluent para-speak, was explaining why modern Thatcherism in relation to the social and economic policies of the Marxist/Leninist-Infiltrated Labour Party and the Communist Greater London Council, provided a more advantageous balance between social and defence expenditure, thereby making available more funds to support the Industrialised Military Complex.

The Lance-Corporal sounded like this: 'That Maggie, she's all right mate, not like those fucking pinko Commies in the Labour Party. Look at that London cunt Ken Livingstone, spendin' all that good money on dirty fuckin' nigger lesbians. You wouldn't get our Maggie doing that. She'd fuck the black dogs right off she would. "Go and score some more ammo for my boys," that's what she'd fuckin' say.'

As I was actually sitting on a ship that was taking me

towards an actual war I found myself feeling some sympathy for the warped logic of the Lance-Corporal's comments.

The Lance-Corporal came to an abrupt halt mid-way through his next sentence. 'What the fuck is that!' he exclaimed.

I turned to look at whatever the LCPL had seen. At the far end of the wide corridor, strutting along, waving, smiling and calling out comments to the soldiers he was passing, was a civvy. A gay civvy. No doubt about that. The corridor broke out into various calls of 'Hello, darling' followed by wolf whistles and offers of unmentionable sexual favours. We had met Wendy.

As the days passed and we got nearer the Islands, Wendy became someone who, like all of us aboard, was 'just there'. He prompted no more comments from people as he passed and slowly he was accepted as one of us. One of us who was going to war.

Wendy also had a talent, a talent that in the end won over even the most bigoted of 'gay haters'. He could play the piano and sing. Each night he would take to the stage in the large continental lounge and to a packed house of dedicated admirers he would play through his complete repertoire.

On our return journey to England we shared the *Norland* with 3 Para, who had originally sailed to the Islands aboard the *Canberra* with one of the Marine Commando battalions. The powers that be realised that they would have a bloodbath on their hands that would make Goose Green look like a picnic if Paras and Marines were sent home together and so 3 Para were put aboard the *Norland* with us.

I can recall sitting in one of the bars playing cards with the usual 'school' plus a couple of 3 Para soldiers who had asked to join us. Wendy walked past and waved a hello. One of the 3 Para soldiers asked who the fuck the dirty little queer was.

I think he wished he hadn't.

The whole table turned on him. He was told that Wendy might be a queer, but he was our fucking queer, and unless he wanted his fucking teeth pushed down his fucking throat, he should shut the fuck up.

The soldier apologised.

Wendy's finest hour was his 'Farewell Tour'. (He played three venues: our bar, the Sergeants' bar and the Officers' bar.) It fell on Airborne Forces Day (which is like paratroopers Christmas), as we sailed towards home. The bar was packed to the limit. As the piano was carried to the stage everyone began stamping their feet and shouting: 'Wendy, Wendy, Wendy.'

He finished each song to roaring applause and was forced to play several encores. Finally, when his songs were finished and the noise had died down, he was presented with one of our coveted Red Berets. He was made an honourable paratrooper.

Everyone had their own little story to tell about Wendy. My favourite is one told by one of the Battalion's SNCOs at the time: 'There I was aboard the *Norland* in San Carlos Bay, fucking Argie jets zooming above my head, the ship's been hit twice, I got some shithead on the radio screaming at me that they need more ammunition at Goose Green, we're all working like slaves to load a landing craft and I've got fucking Wendy beasting me to get a fucking move on. Fifteen fucking years I've waited for this, and when it does finally happen I've got some gay boy leaning over me telling ME to fucking hurry up because HIS boys are running out of fucking ammo.'

Today, whenever I meet or speak to soldiers from my battalion and we reminisce about the Falklands War, Wendy always gets a mention. In fact it is true to say that he now gets more of a mention than the likes of Colonel Jones VC. Whether this is wrong or right, I do not know. But it is true. And no longer is Wendy referred to as an arse bandit, or a turd burglar or a dirty fucking queer. Gay boy's about the worst you will hear and it's always said with a smile, it's always said with affection.

You see, we do live – and we can learn.

Things you never knew about war
(No. 23)

The whole world goes religious on you.

It started on the boat down. The nearer we got the higher the attendances. By the time we got to the service before the service before the service before we landed, God was playing to a full house.

I read in a book that at these church services we, the men of the Second Battalion, The Parachute Regiment, were given the opportunity to stand together before God and each other as equals. I read in another book that when the clock struck midnight Cinderella lost her glass slipper and the carriage turned back into a pumpkin. (I ask myself this: if we're all equal before God, then how come on war memorials in churches the names of the officers are always engraved above the names of the other ranks?)

It seemed like everyone was going to church. Except for me. I didn't go.

I had been raised as a Jehovah's Witness, so gathering with others and having a good old natter about God was something I had done three times weekly until I was about fifteen. You can say a lot about the Jehovah's Witnesses but, credit where credit's due, they do know their bible and they do live by their bible, and from what I've read about the teachings of Christ I do believe that's the general idea if it's everlasting life the Christian way you're after.

The followers of the teachings of Christ known as the Jehovah's Witnesses (hereinafter referred to as the JWs) don't go a lot on war: they're pacifists – it's something to do with the bit in their version of the bible that reads 'Thou shalt not kill.' The followers of the teachings of Christ known as the Church of England Military Chaplains (hereinafter referred to as the MOD C of E) are not pacifists – I believe that this has something to do with the bit in their *revised* version of the bible that reads 'Thou shalt not murder.'

Because of my religiously-based pacifist upbringing I always had a problem coming to terms with the Church within the Army. Priests in soldier-suits blessing regimental colours while happily praising the Lord was something I found strange. I think I was just having trouble coming to terms with, on the one hand learning to kill people, and on the other telling Jesus all about it.

This, of course, was being far too harsh on the MOD C of E: after all, why shouldn't two mediaeval institutions walk through time together, holding hands, continually helping to reaffirm each other's presence? For all I know Jesus might even like the idea. He does love us all – and that's in both versions.

On the morning of the first day in Goose Green settlement, shortly after we had released the local inhabitants from their confinement, I met and spoke to our battalion padre, Captain Cooper. I can recall saying to him that the events of the past couple of days had made me start to think about God, that they had increased my faith in him. The padre replied that that was strange, because the last few days had had the opposite effect on him, his faith had been shaken. He then walked off. For some reason the padre's comments made me feel small. I wished I had kept my mouth shut. When I had said that my faith had been strengthened by witnessing a battle I had not been speaking the truth. I had said what I thought the padre might like to hear.

On the other hand, I may have said what I wanted to believe. Don't know.

The first prayer meet on the Islands for us Christian soldiers of the eighties was held at Goose Green, two days after the battle. Nice turnout we had as well. Even I went. There was lots of 'Greater love hath no man than this, that a man lay down his life for his friends,' etc. A few hymns, a quick rendition of the Lord's Prayer, a few requests to the Almighty to please guide us safely through whatever comes our way tomorrow. Amens all round and off we all went back to our trenches to prepare ourselves for the slaying of a few more Catholics.

Made a nice change. Helped to break the routine.

In Fitzroy, while there were still only a few of us there, I held a church service. A group of us were living in a workshop that was part of a large sheep shed, but partitioned off from the rest of the shed's interior. Our group mainly consisted of soldiers from the battalion's Assault Engineer Platoon. The platoon had only recently been re-formed and all of its members, bar its three NCOs, had only been with the battalion for a few months.

The Assault Engineer Platoon was not only the newest in the battalion, its members were also the youngest. One of them had not yet turned eighteen. He used to ponder aloud: 'How the fuck is it all right for me to go off to war and yet I can't vote, can't drink in pubs and am not allowed to see X films because they might be too violent for me?'

I would always tell him to look on the bright side. Should he get killed he would always remain in regimental history, and no doubt in the nation's history, as the youngest British soldier ever to have been killed during a Tory Party electoral campaign.

To this he would always reply: 'Why don't you fuck off and die.'

My church service for the members of the Assault Engineer Platoon took the form of a Deep South (as in *Gone with the Wind*) bible-belt, born-again, pentecostal-type meeting.

I walked into the room with Ray in tow and in my best Deep-South American accent, asked my brothers to, 'Say Hallelujah, Praise the Lord.'

They all replied, 'Hallelujah, Praise the Lord.'

'Dear Brothers, would ya please bow your heads and join with me in the saying of our Lord's Prayer:

'Our Mother, who art in Downing Street, Hollow be Thy Party Manifesto, Thy will be done in Brixton as it is in Richmond-upon-Thames. Give us each day our daily resupply of Ammunition and forgive us our negligent discharges even though we don't forgive those bastards who negligently discharge against us. Lead us not into minefields, and deliver us from the Regimental Sergeant-Major. Amen.'

A touch disrespectful, I agree. But you got to have a laugh.

The day after we arrived in Port Stanley our battalion held a proper church service. We all washed and shaved, made smart our clothing as best we could, and as a battalion marched through the streets of Stanley and into the cathedral.

It was let's play Hero Para time again.

The service was filmed by a TV crew. I have a video-tape copy of the service. I can recognise myself standing in one of the back rows. I always joke to myself that when I die, should it turn out that the Christians were right, then I can always show the videotape in my defence.

As I stood in the cathedral, I found myself looking at the faces of the men around me. I had the thought that we were all now very different to how we had been a few weeks before. We had seen a war. I thought that we were all now better people for having seen it. That not one of us could ever go back to being whatever we had been before. We wouldn't bully, we would never strike the first blow, we would be compassionate, more respectful towards women. As I thought, the padre talked: 'What I would ask you to remember, is what you felt when you thought you were going to die, and what was important to you then? It may have been your wife, it may have been your girlfriend, it may have been your dog.'

On hearing the word 'dog' a few amongst us began to chuckle. The chuckles spread and grew into laughter.

The padre continued: 'It may even . . .' He had to pause because of more laughter. The slow ones amongst us had just got the 'dog' joke. '. . . it may even have been your life itself.'

So much for my thought about respecting women . . .

I have often thought about what the padre asked of us. Who had we thought of when we were going to die? For me the answer was my mother. If I had been the padre I would have liked to have asked another question. I would have asked this: 'Who had you thought of when you knew you were going to live, and what was important to you then?'

I had thought of ME. It was ME who was important to me then.

At the church service in Port Stanley, after the war, we gave thanks to God for our deliverance from death. We also asked him to care for the loved ones of the dead. We thanked the Lord, though we never once asked forgiveness.

But I've asked a few times since.

I like to think that I know my bible. I was forced to read it as a child, and there was also a period of time when I was Born Again as it was once put to my old mate Nicodemus.

I had always believed that as a Christian your life is dictated by the example set by Christ. That a Christian should try to live his life as Christ lived his. With this as the basis to all thought, all action, I ask myself: what would Christ have done if he had been at Goose Green? I like to believe that he would have asked his fellow man to lay down his gun. Not to take another life. To take his instead.

Maybe I've understood it all wrong.

I shall remember them
(sometimes)

Since the Falklands War I have often gone into British Legion Clubs. On the wall in most of them there is a plaque. On the plaque these words are inscribed:

At the going down of the sun, and in the morning
We shall remember them.'

For me these words are a lie. When I awake each day my mind does not recall the dead that I once knew. I am usually occupied with thoughts of how I am going to pay the outstanding bills I have pinned to my kitchen wall or what the day before me will hold. At night as I lay my head on my pillow I seldom recall the dead that I once knew. I am normally trying to understand the confusion I have created around my life over the past nine years, as I watch vivid mental replays of my past insanities.

At the end of the evening, in the rooms with plaques on the walls, all the old soldiers stand to attention and, in the same way an actor recites an author's lines, they say aloud the words that are inscribed on the plaques. I look around the rooms at the faces of the old soldiers and wonder if they might also be lying? My own hypocrisy disturbs me, for I know that as long as the majority of us continue to act out the plays that have been written for us by the politicians, their priests and the men of this world who control the money, then we shall never be able to put an end to the horrors of war.

I do remember the dead that I once knew, the dead on both sides of the war that I fought in. But I remember them not with the part of me that sits drunk amongst old soldiers and brags of the glories of war, but with the part of me that has seen a war, knows of its true horror, the stupidity of it, and still feels an inner unrest for having witnessed it.

I do remember the dead that I once knew, but not with the part of me that loudly shouts, 'What about the filthy spick fucker that the sarge blew away?' but with the part of me that when in solitude, whispers a prayer for the one-eyed, dying boy from the Argentine.

I do remember the dead that I once knew, but not with the part of me that speaks of brave young men who charged to a heroic death, a death for the Queen, a death for a just cause, a death for their country. But with the part of me that tells of the young men who had their flesh ripped and punctured by flying metal, young men who screamed and died in agony, young men who prayed for mercy, prayed for mercy to a God they had never accepted before.

You see, I do remember the dead that I once knew – sometimes.

I would like to change the inscriptions on the plaques. I would like to be able to give myself a chance of being truthful. I would write these words instead:

'Sometimes – when we are able to find our true selves – we shall remember them.'